AN OPEN MARKET FOR INFORMAL WORKERS:
THE PRECARIOUS LABOUR CHOWKS OF DELHI

AN OPEN MARKET FOR INFORMAL WORKERS:
THE PRECARIOUS LABOUR CHOWKS OF DELHI

Jenny Sulfath and Shirin Choudhary

YODA PRESS
79 Gulmohar Enclave
New Delhi 110 049
www.yodapress.co.in

ISBN 978-93-82579-83-0

Editors in charge: Soumya Jayanti and Himadri Agarwal
Typeset in Adobe Minion Pro, 11/14.4
By MSourcing
Published by Arpita Das for YODA PRESS

Contents

Preface

This study on labour chowk was imagined as a collaborative effort between the research team of Centre For Equity Studies (CES) and the field team of Hausla, a programme under CES which is exclusively working on the rights of the urban homeless. CES runs two shelter homes in Delhi; one of them in Yamuna Pushta predominantly shelters workers from the labour chowks who are homeless. The observations of the patterns of employment by the field team closely working with them helped shape this study. The field research team initially consisted of Satyaveer Singh Yadav from Hausla and Jenny Sulfath, one of the co-authors of this report. Satyaveer arrived in New Delhi as a homeless child. He used to get work from the labour chowks in *shaadi* parties. He later worked with various civil society organizations on the issue of homelessness and the rights of the urban poor. The fieldwork was later joined by Sachin, a resident of the shelter home, and Ramzan, an employee at the shelter home. Their familiarity with the space and people immensely helped in the data collection process of this study.

For this report, we employed multiple methods of data collection. Initially, the team visited 13 labour chowks to map the employment conditions of workers, and their wellbeing. These visits to the labour chowk were made in the mornings. Though we intended to document their experiences through in-depth interviews, the methods employed eventually were mostly conversational and non-participant observations. Since the workers wait in groups to get assigned, conducting in-depth interviews was difficult, since people would get picked up in the middle of the interviews, and they were also reluctant to reveal their names or other details for fear of being identified by the other workers. Some of them were embarrassed about living in the streets and about the other villagers back home finding out, while others were actively hiding from their families due to personal issues, land disputes or police cases, and most of them did not trust each other to share their caste or religious details fearing unwanted attention and discrimination. A few days into the data collection, the conversations were getting increasingly repetitive. The study then focused specifically on two labour chowks: Sarai Kale Khan labour chowk in South Delhi, and Company Baug labour chowk in Central Delhi. Because the workers at Company Baug labour chowk mostly lived in the shelter homes of Yamuna Pushta (embankment), it was easier to visit and speak to them at length when they were not at work. One of the residents of the shelter home was trained to conduct the interviews and assist in data collection. The street medicine team of CES regularly visited the Sarai Kale Khan labour chowk at night and accompanying them on these visits helped us establish a relationship of trust with our respondents. Since the visits were made at night, the workers staying at the chowk were also able to spend more time talking to us, compared to the mornings, when they are desperately looking for work. One obvious limitation of this methodology is that, given the transitory nature of the population, and that they do not carry mobile phones for fear of theft, follow-up interviews were not possible.

In addition to documenting the experience of the workers, the study was also intended to understand the general profile of the workers: who does what kinds of work and the general conditions in which they live. To adequately represent their conditions, a survey was conducted in these two labour chowks and 430 samples were collected. It should be noted that the data might not represent the condition of workers at all the labour chowks in Delhi. Out of all the respondents from the two labour chowks, only 7 out of 430 were born in Delhi. Most of them were migrants. Additionally, we also used a GPS app to map the Sarai Kale Khan labour chowk, in order to adequately understand spatial inequality: how much space a worker is allowed to access and how their location subsequently determines the unequal access to resources.

This study benefited immensely from the guidance and mentorship of Dr. Harsh Mander at every stage. We extend our gratitude towards Dr. Mythri Prasad-Aleyamma and Ashwin Parulkar for their inputs in developing the research questions. Our colleague Dr. Anirban Bhattacharya's comments and feedbacks helped structure this study at each stage. We are grateful to Ruzel Shreshta for his assistance in analysing the quantitative data. We are also extremely grateful to our colleagues Shruti Iyer, Armaan Alkazi, Buddhadeb Halder and others for their support. The assistance of our interns Amna, Ishtikar, Asma, Lochan, Mark, Shamik, and Lakshita in data collection requires special acknowledgement.

1

Introduction

Delhi is known for its small road-side eateries and restaurants that serve low-cost food. A considerable number of people employed at these eateries (commonly known as *dhabas*) come from Delhi's Company Baug labour chowk. Hundreds of workers, even thousands during peak season, gather around a park in Old Delhi early in the morning, looking for work. Many of these workers live on footpaths and shelter homes near the chowk. Those who live further away walk several kilometres to the labour chowk, seeking work for their everyday sustenance. Homeless migrants in Delhi work at dhabas doing '*paani pyaaz*' work, i.e., serving food, cleaning tables, supplying the tables with onion slices and water, and washing the dishes (also known colloquially as *masalchi*). This work gives them food to eat and a place to sleep at night. Restaurants and dhabas prefer to hire homeless persons because one, they are cheap labour, and two, they work non-stop till they go to sleep. Even big hotels rely on them in peak seasons when they have insufficient in-house staff.

Another thriving industry in this ever-expanding city is the construction sector. The built geography of Delhi is changing every day with the mushrooming of new flyovers and skyscrapers. The city itself continues to engulf more and more of its rural surroundings, broadening the boundaries of the 'National Capital Region' (NCR). This expansion relies on the large migrant workforce, both old and new, to construct these large spacious buildings, even as they themselves sleep on footpaths, in labour camps, and in cramped rooms in *bastis* and resettlement colonies. Every day, contractors throng the labour chowks, hiring workers to build this city.

The workers who come to the labour chowks regularly face many difficulties. They grapple with the precarity of irregular work in a daily wage economy, long working hours, wage theft, and the lack of secure housing and sanitation. Consequent exclusion from welfare measures, both at the source and destination of their migration, compounds their vulnerabilities. Most women workers reported having to work during pregnancy, and a complete absence of workplace institutions for proper child-care. Housing precarity underpins other forms of exclusion workers experience, since proof of address is a prerequisite to exercise any rights and avail welfare measures in the status quo. Discrimination on the basis of disability, landlessness, caste, mental health status, gender, marital status, and several other factors further marginalizes them, and hinders their everyday survival.

This report outlines the work practices and experiences of workers from different labour chowks to understand the nature of their work. Further, it explores everyday life, reasons for migration, challenges, vulnerabilities, discriminations faced, etc. through their narratives. It then presents, through a survey of reports, a general profile of the workers at the labour chowk. The last part of our report discusses gaps in existing policies and laws which lead to the exclusion of workers and prevent them from accessing justice, which is followed by a section on spatial inequalities. The study is primarily an attempt to reimagine how spaces emerge as a tool to understand labour, and how the production of knowledge on specific occupational groups should be attentive to spaces and mobility to develop inclusive policies. The current legal framework assumes vertical uniformity across different groups of wage labourers; their patterns of mobility and the vulnerability due to them should be a central focus while designing policies.

1.1. Recruitment Practices in the Catering and Hotel Industry: Insights from Company Baug Labour Chowk

The Company Baug labour chowk in Old Delhi is a labour chowk from where workers are hired exclusively to work at restaurants, banquet halls, and farmhouses during the wedding season. Big restaurants generally recruit their in-house staff directly from remote, poor regions of India for abysmally low wages. Substitutes for these workers are brought in from among the readily available labour pool in Company Baug who are given slightly higher wages. The Company Baug chowk also provides a pool of workers to dhabas, which recruit workers for a prolonged period. During Delhi's wedding season, workers also take up catering work at farmhouses and banquet halls.

In catering, the more interactive labour, that involves greeting people, serving food, etc. is carried out by well-groomed young workers, while the more invisible and underpaid work, like loading and unloading the crockery, setting up the furniture, chopping vegetables for the feast, making hot rotis on demand, clearing tables, washing dishes and packing up the entire place, is done by the Company Baug workers. If the wedding goes on for days, the workers are expected to work on all days without proper rest. Two days of almost non-stop work with only a short break will fetch a worker an average of Rs. 1,500. Rates vary based on seasonal demands; there are days when they get as little as Rs. 250 for an entire day of work. Despite these long working hours and low pay, workers prefer wedding parties because there, they get free food. This helps them save some money to send back home.

The chowk is controlled by three or four agents (known as *dalaals*) who earn through the commission they charge employers and contractors. Ravi Tyagi, one of the dhaba workers, informed us that the contractors charge Rs. 50 per worker for engagements in Delhi and Rs. 100–150 per person for work in Gurgaon and other areas within the NCR. *It is nothing but the buying and selling of humans.* The meaning of these words would become clearer to us when we heard from the workers about their days at some of these dhabas.

> Apart from being a space where workers gather to look for work, the Company Baug labour chowk is also where some workers live. The dhabas which give them cheap food during the day double up as spaces for them to sleep in at night. Some also spend their nights at the shelter homes close by. Many such workers rely on the shelter homes in Yamuna Pushta, an important site of engagement for this study. It was previously a settlement of workers who were later evicted in 2004 following a PIL in the Delhi High Court. It now houses homeless people in shelter homes built by the government and run by various NGOs. Munna, who used to live in Yamuna Pushta in his own *jhuggi* (shanty), recounts how this space has changed over the years: It had a population of five lakhs. It was spread till Shantivan. Now everyone is scattered. That place has become a park now. They had settled there during Indira Gandhi's time, I think. Some people ran hotels and small businesses. Everything is finished now. The place was burnt down several times, mainly during the election season. Many people left for ITO after that, many went to Dhaula Kuan. Everyone was scattered. You will find a lot of girls (from here) in Chandni Chowk who pick cardboard from waste.

In very simple words, Munna explains how the working class in Delhi was dispossessed from even basic necessities. The *bastis* were a political subject during the elections. Munna recollects that there was an eviction drive in 2001 when the metro was being inaugurated. The settlement caught fire once again and police were deployed to evict them. When his jhuggi was lost in the eviction drives, Munna moved to the shelter home that sprang up simultaneously, while his sister moved with her family to Bawana, where they were resettled.

Gautham Bhan (2017) traces the history of Yamuna Pushta in his book, *In the Public's Interest: Evictions, Citizenship and Inequality in Contemporary Delhi.* He notes that between February and April 2004, in a series of operations carried out by armed police, the Yamuna Pushta settlement was demolished. Out of the people evicted from the Pushta, only 30% households were rehabilitated in Bawana. Munna's sister and her family lived in a single jhuggi, and they constructed a separate shed for Munna. It was only his sister's family that was enlisted for rehabilitation, while his name was left out. Through processes like this, where the household was defined in the most limited fashion, dispossession of homes and the network they built around them was compounded and cemented.

From most worker testimonies, it is clear that Yamuna Pushta continues to serve as shelter for many migrant workers who arrive in the city with no place to go. Despite being disentitled to the area and having no legal claim to it whatsoever, some migrants still live under the Yamuna bridge, especially in summers as the Delhi heat soars. While some of them are rickshaw pullers and vendors, a considerable number of them are dependent on the nearby labour chowks for work.

Recruitment for wedding parties and catering sometimes takes place directly from the Pushta area. Cell phone owners benefit from being in constant touch with *thekedars* (contractors), since the *thekedars* tend to directly contact workers to hire them. However, due to lack of options for safekeeping of their valuables, several workers report having their phones stolen. Bereft of a phone, the labour chowk becomes their only channel to scout for work.

Rahul Kumar[1] goes to the Company Baug labour chowk for work and lives in a shelter home in Yamuna Pushta. He wakes up at 6 AM and walks to the labour chowk. He drinks tea in the morning only if he has Rs. 5–10 with him. Reaching the labour chowk at 8 AM means that it is too late to find work. The only jobs left are the low-paying ones. Employers from faraway places arrive early since they need workers to run their establishments later in the morning. They also pay better than those who come later. Rahul waits at the labour chowk till 10 or 10:30 AM, after which very

---

1 Interview taken in February 2019

few people come to hire workers. If he does not get work, he eats at the Gurudwara or Mandir. A full account of Rahul's struggle with the daily labour appears later in this report.

At the chowk, the *dalaals* (agents) sit in a tarpaulin tent, as the workers crowd around. Employers and contractors directly approach the dalaals, who then announce the work and the offered wage. Workers who agree with the wage compete to be picked up.

As mentioned earlier, the dalaals charge a commission of Rs. 50–150, based on where the workers are being taken. Those looking to hire from the chowk are either owners of small dhabas in Delhi, *thekedars* for big hotels, or the assistants of owners of dhabas on the highway in Haryana. Wedding party contractors also hire at the chowk seasonally.

1.2.   Labour Process in Dhabas and Wedding Party Work

Dhaba work has its own division of labour. Dish washers are considered entry-level workers and are usually the inexperienced ones. Depending on their efficiency, the owners sometimes move people to work that involves directly interacting with the customers. This is commonly referred to as *service ka kaam*. However, the recognition of efficiency often leads to just more work and less reward. Rahul was asked by his boss to leave a portion of his wages to ensure that he would return to the same place for work. Nevertheless, he decided to never return to the same workplace.

The workers from the labour chowk are employed for different types of informal work associated with the catering industry. The same work is also carried out by ventures and agencies with a more formal work arrangement with their workers. According to the respondents, some recruiting companies specifically take up the contract for loading and unloading work. When they need extra workers beyond their regular ones, they hire people from the labour chowks. The farmhouse weddings mostly need loading and unloading labour. Banquet halls have their own permanent arrangements for seating and serving. When loading and unloading is included in the work, the wages are higher; in banquet halls, the wages are lower. The working shifts also do not have a fixed time in wedding party work. The night-time is spent mostly on moving and setting up the place, while the day is spent cooking and serving. These schedules also change depending on the time of the party. These wage differentials based on the nature of work, time, intensity, and seasonality are often not accounted for when the wage limits are set in order to define who is a migrant worker and who is not.

Raju[2], a migrant worker from Siliguri, explains why workers run away from dhaba work. Raju was hired at a dhaba in Chhatarpur from the Company Baug labour chowk. He recounts that the work would stretch from 7 AM to midnight. Raju and his co-workers would get to eat only after this and then would finally get to lie down at around 1:30-2 AM, after which they would take another hour to fall asleep. Raju describes his work as extremely tiring and, more importantly, unending.

The interview with Raju also brought up similar points about the practices in hotel and catering related work. The rates are not standardised at all in the labour chowk. The same work which is paid Rs. 1,500 can go as low as Rs. 400 in off seasons. The work commitment is temporary. The agreement between the workers and the contractors are often not honoured. If the employers find someone to be hardworking, they keep a part of their wage to themselves so that the workers come back to get it and keep working there. More often than not, the workers lose this money. The shift in the dhabas extends up to 18 hours while there is no fixed wage for fixed hours. The desperation of the workers determines the wage and working hours. Most of the workers have pointed out that after long hours of work, they do not get enough sleep because they must wake up early. Consuming alcohol is the only way to

---

2 Interview taken in January 2019

pass out and sleep in small, restricted spaces. A detailed account of Raju's experiences is mentioned in the upcoming section.

These informal recruitment practices are exploitative, and the labour processes are taxing. Agents take zero responsibility for the workers' well-being. Moreover, the workers are not told in advance about the nature of commitment or the length of their working days. Sometimes, they are told that the agents have taken money for a longer time than they had anticipated and hence, they are bound to work for longer periods of time than previously agreed upon, for a wage agreed upon by the agents and the employer.

Recruitment directly from the labour chowk is one of many modes of recruitment. Catering as an industry employs different kinds of workers, all of whom are informal workers. Some of them are permanent workers—they are hired for fixed monthly wages and promised work for longer terms. However, this does not mean they have a formal contract. Some are recruited through third party agencies supplying labour for specific tasks, and some are hired from the labour chowks. The mode of payment, whether task-based short-term wage or employment-based monthly wage, determines the informal channel through which the workers get recruited. It benefits the catering industry to have a fixed number of low-paid workers for continuous employment and a dispensable mass of workers from the labour chowk during seasons of high demand.

1.3. Labour Recruitment in Construction: Insights from Sarai Kale Khan and Other Labour Chowks

Yet another set of migrants arrive in the city and gather around at another labour chowk in South Delhi outside the Hazrat Nizamuddin Railway Station. They are mostly agrarian migrant workers who arrive seasonally at the Sarai Kale Khan labour chowk with their families to work in Delhi's construction sector. They occupy the chowk along with other homeless people, beggars, and street hawkers for a few days and move to their workplaces when they find work. The more permanent occupants of the chowk are beggars, who find work at times, and come back to the labour chowk to sleep at night. Workers get recruited for minor maintenance work, demolition of buildings, and as *beldars* (those who do excavation work) in the organized construction sector. This sector mainly relies on mass recruitment from Adivasi communities and other vulnerable communities from remote areas. The workers from the labour chowk are hired by subcontractors for seasonal requirements. The differences between the more permanent workers and the labour chowk workers are that one, the workers recruited from the village receive an advance, and two, they get continuous employment for a prolonged duration through one single contractor. On the other hand, the workers from the labour chowk are recruited for specific tasks if there is a shortage of workers. Similar to the hotel industry, the workers from the labour chowk are paid slightly better than the mass-recruited migrants. The availability of these dispensable workers ensures the continuity of work without being bound by the responsibilities of providing them minimal security (basic housing, water etc.).

Anees,[3] a petty contractor working in East Kidwai Nagar explains the difference between the two kinds of informal workers employed at the East Kidwai Nagar construction site:

> Anees: People come from Bengal and Jharkhand to work at the construction site. They are recruited directly from their villages. The company asks the *jamadars* (jobbers) to go and get helpers, and they bring on workers for 60 days, paying them Rs. 6,000 a month.

> Interviewer: Isn't it too low?

> Anees: But the thekedar pays for their travel from the village to the construction sites. He also pays for food and accommodation. They are called supply labour: they clean up the site after work, carry concrete from one floor to another, etc. The *jamadar* takes a commission of Rs. 50 per person. The thekedar gets Rs. 375 per person from the company.

---

3 Interview taken in February 2019

Anees then goes on to explain why the workers are willing to accept such a low wage in his understanding:

> Because they do not have any work there, no? They have mountains and forests. What kind of work will they do there in forests? And they need to eat. When the jamadar goes to their homes, he makes the payment in advance. He pays Rs. 6,000, Rs. 7,000, Rs. 8,000, and so on. So, when they see all that money at once, they get happy and send their children here to work.

Even though Anees's narration reflects his own relatively dominant position as an urban non-Adivasi petty contractor, it also shows the other end of mass dispossession the Adivasis continue to face. While India has a history of indentured labour recruited from Adivasi regions to plantations in colonial times, a similar process is ongoing today with a different format of recruitment in the construction sector. The middlemen and thekedars pay these young workers from the tribal areas abysmally low wages. Since they are young and mostly women workers, and the payment is made to their parents, their mobility in the city is restricted. They are placed at the lowest rung of the construction sector. According to Anees, while the jamadar directly takes a commission from the thekedars, the thekedar pays a much lower wage to the workers.

The presence and recruitment of these workers adversely affects the recruitment of the other workers at the labour chowk. Earlier, the construction sector was largely dependent on these workers who would return to the labour chowk daily after work. Now, a larger portion of the work goes mostly to the mass-recruited workers. A common response to the question of issues at work was 'there is no work these days.'

Workers from the labour chowk are now employed by large construction sites such as East Kidwai Nagar only in emergency situations. They are hired strictly for a day or night's work where the wages are settled by the end of the day. Compared to 'supply labour' or regular labour, the workers from the labour chowk are better paid. The 'helpers' are paid Rs. 350 and skilled workers are paid Rs. 450 per day. However, the disadvantage of this recruitment system is that the thekedar claims wages for more people than are sent to work. The amount of work remains the same. The supervisors get a commission to not report this to the company. If there is an inspection, they quickly get a few more people from the nearby chowk to avoid getting caught. The work, in essence, becomes harder for the workers in this case. Since the company or the contractors do not need to think about the health of the workers (because they are not useful to them for a prolonged period), their labour power is exploited more. Ultimately, even if they are better paid for a day, their days are laborious.

The workers we met at the labour chowk represented a mixed demography. They were predominantly men, but from across various caste backgrounds. However, from Anees's narrative, the 'supply labour' is mostly Adivasis and young women. He says:

> Ahirs and Yadavs do not know any work other than construction and agriculture. When they cannot make enough money from agriculture, they come to the city and look for work in construction. They work for daily wages and wait for contractors at the labour chowk. Adivasis who live in the hills don't know any work. They go to the forest and collect firewood. When they need money, they send their children to cities.

The workers who are directly recruited by building companies through agents are often from the most backward castes and regions. Single men from the agrarian middle castes have the slight advantage of looking for work on their own as opposed to being dependent on the recruiters at the source. This allows them to bargain directly for a slightly higher wage from the labour chowk. The 'advantage' of this system is that it keeps the wages in check. If there is a demand for higher wages from the regular workers, the ready availability of workers in labour chowks curbs such demands.

The families that arrive at the labour chowk are also hired to work in the construction sector for prolonged periods of time.

Those who come to Delhi carrying mobile phones call the thekedar they might have worked for earlier, so he can come pick them up. Otherwise, they wait at the labour chowk for the thekedar to arrive. The eldest and more experienced member of the family negotiates with the thekedar. Since they are a family, they prefer a jhuggi in the labour camp and agree to work for a smaller monthly wage rather than a higher daily wage. The better the jhuggi is (the quality of the jhuggi being computed from availability of water, electricity, and bathrooms), the lower the wage. The priority of the family is to be employed as a group rather than being split up in multiple sites. The thekedars come from the peripheries of the NCR, mostly from Haryana or Greater Noida. Some of the workers are taken to bigger, organized construction sites. If there is one *mistri* (skilled worker) in the group, they are also hired for smaller construction sites. In that case, the family also lives in the same building.

1.4.   Labour Process in the Construction Sector

The labour process—what work one is assigned, how long one works, wages, and their rank in the workplace hierarchy—is predetermined by gender and age. The nature and duration of work depends on the skills required and the worksite as well. The construction sector is large and diversified.

In our conversations with the families in Sarai Kale Khan, we were told that once a family arrives at the construction site, they receive an initial advance. The advance is meant for the family to set up a jhuggi, get firewood, set up the kitchen, purchase basics such as buckets, utensils etc. Some of the families carry their own gas stove and utensils from their village. Single men have to share a jhuggi or room with other men.

There are multiple shifts in big construction sites. In practice, women and men take up different work shifts. Women wake up early in the morning, cook for the family, fetch water, feed the children, and then leave for work. They are also expected to arrive early and set up the place before the *mistri* arrives. Their main task is to assist the masons; they are responsible for mixing cement, carrying the concrete to different floors, filling the tank with water, keeping the tools in place, etc. Unskilled men are next in the hierarchy bottom up. These comprise mostly of young men, travelling with neighbours or extended family, hoping to learn skilled work. Older men also work as helpers. The skilled workers are all men, having acquired these skills by assisting a senior labourer for years. The skilled labourers sometimes become masons, or thekedars. This upward trajectory in the informal hierarchy, however, is rare.

If one is recruited for a single day, they reach the workplace with the thekedars, or in a vehicle arranged by the thekedar. Depending on their skill set, they are made to work for the entire day.

Most of the workers rarely prefer to work in smaller or individual construction sites from Sarai Kale Khan. Despite being seasonal workers, because most of them arrive with their families with at least one female member, they prefer to go to the bigger construction sites that offer them a place to stay. However, in chowks where the workers are more local, they pick up task-based work such as electrical repairing or plumbing for a task-based rate of Rs. 100–200.

Masons, plumbers, and electricians get Rs. 500–700 in daily wages. Wages are determined by skill set, the nature of the construction site, and the desperation of the workers, among other factors. The owners themselves come to pick up workers for smaller sites, demolition, and maintenance work. Owners do not offer a full day's wage for maintenance work. The workers told us that they sometimes end up having to work for longer hours than they were previously told, but the owners refuse to pay them overtime wages, blaming the delay on their inefficiency. The workers also reported instances of owners denying them their wages on the pretext of poor quality of work. On the other hand, bigger construction sites are largely consistent in paying the daily wages of day labourers.

2

Locating the Workers of the Labour Chowk in Labour Migration in India

The scholarship on migration has focused on various sectors where migrant workers are employed to understand mobility of labour. A detailed and in-depth study was done by Jan Breman (2016) in his book *On Pauperism in Present and Past*, which discussed the lives of the labour chowk workers (referred to as *nakka* workers in his chapter) in Gujarat. His observations are useful in identifying the role of land ownership in placing workers from various social locations and identities on the spectrum of migration. For example, he observes that there is a inverse correlation between the number of women in labour camps and *nakkas*, and the extent of landholding in each family. Landless workers bring their families with them to the city, whereas for the landed workers, it is important to leave the women home to take care of cattle and agriculture. He further notes that the landless workers remain in the labour camps or urban settlements for longer periods as compared to the land-owning migrants who return to their village seasonally. According to the study, the landless labourers no longer return home to work, even if they have a dwelling back in the village. The lack of social capital to find better jobs keeps them moving from one place to another. However, they are never able to find a foothold in the urban economy.

In describing the workers who live near labour chowks, on footpaths and in night shelters and dependent on *nakkas* for work, he argues that it is inaccurate to describe the movement of this set of footloose workers as migration, as they are never able to establish a foothold where they move. In his opinion, what is often described as migration should in fact be termed circulation. (ibid) While migration to urban areas is a result of the agrarian crisis and the lack of adequate employment in rural areas, he also observes that their attempt to be permanent in-migrants in the city is challenged by the saturation of employment and the reluctance of the well-settled urban inhabitants to tolerate the presence of poor people in their midst (Breman, 2010).

To bolster this, Manish K Jha and Pushpendra Kumar (2016) have pointed out that a large number of labour migrants in urban areas belong to poor working classes. Unable to access proper housing in the city, they are forced to live in public spaces or at the worksite. Jha and Kumar (ibid) have drawn from the definition of homelessness by the United Nations, understanding it to be the state of not only those who live on the streets or in shelters, but also those whose housing fails to fulfil basic requirements considered essential for health and social development. This includes security of tenure, protection against weather, personal security, access to sanitary facilities, potable water, education, health, and work (Speak and Tipple 2006, as quoted by Jha and Kumar 2016).

Breman (ibid) characterizes the *nakka* not simply as a meeting place for daily recruitment but also a transit point for the workers to follow up on previously agreed upon deals with the contractors. While there are workers who would come to a *nakka* looking for fresh work, some workers who are directly employed by contractors for a longer term also come there to find work when there is a gap (of a few days) between assignments.

Nivedita Jayaram, Priyanka Jain, and Sangeeth S Sugathan's work on migrant Adivasi women labourers in Ahmedabad (2019) also focuses partly on labour *nakkas* in the city, where Adivasi families migrate to the city looking for work in the burgeoning construction industry. The Bhil Adivasi community, having arrived in Ahmedabad looking for work after being displaced from their land, faces multi-layered precarity in the city. Their work in the city is characterized by low wages, lack of access to social capital in the form of support from patrons or neighbours, or access to collective bargaining systems like traditional trade unions, and barriers to any claims over space in the city, as they are often forced to live in 'open spaces across the city and its peripheries.'(ibid) These spaces are riddled with the lack of basic services like toilets, clean water, and cooking fuel. They also live under 'constant scrutiny... with the fear of being evicted and displaced.' (ibid). These factors, argue Jayaram et al., ensure that the working and living conditions for daily wage labourers who live and find work at labour *nakkas* are not much better than the conditions they left behind when they migrated.

Based on a sample of workers from the labour chowks of Delhi, CSK Singh (2002) argues that these labourers represent the *pauperisation of the peasantry*, and it is distress migration rather than the Harris-Torranto model[4] of choice migration, considering the rural-urban wage differential and the calculation of net gains. Focusing on labour *nakkas* and associated workspaces, the work of Breman and CSK Singh points out the limitations of the conventional conceptualization of migration in understanding labour nakkas/chowks.

Definitions of migration as per the two major data sources in India—the decennial population census and the quinquennial migration surveys carried out by the NSSO—exclude the labour chowk workers from the wealth of data it produces on migration. This is partially addressed by the work of Jayaram et al. in their work on Bhil Adivasi migrant women workers, which has pointed

---

4 Two fundamental propositions put forward by this model are that migration is an economically rational optimizing behaviour to maximize their expected gains, and that the urban informal sector is a temporary reservoir for the migrants.

to the fact that families from this community who work as casual labour in the construction industry in Ahmedabad are 'highly mobile' and constantly shifting from their rural source and urban work destinations. They have thus laid bare the gaps in development research and practice, which only focuses on semi-settled or permanent migrants (Jayaram, Jain & Sugathan, 2019).

As per the Census of India, internal migration includes any movement within the political boundaries of a nation which results in a change of 'place of birth' or 'the last place of residence.' If the place of birth or last place of residence is different from the place of enumeration, a person is defined as a migrant (Srivastava). The NSS confines itself to the Usual Place of Residence (UPR) definition. In both the surveys, a resident is defined as one who has been staying in a location for six months or more (except newly born infants) (ibid).

Workers who come to the labour chowk often go back to their native villages several times within six months and are hence likely to be excluded from the definition of a migrant. Since the workers have precarious residential arrangements in the city, a mode of residence-based definition is inadequate to understand their mobility and labour. The limitation of the Indian statistical system is that it is unequipped to capture the short-term/seasonal/circular migration (Deshingkar and Akter, 2009). However, Jan Breman (2010) suggests that at least 50 million people are and remain on the move in order to make up for the income deficit in their households. Various reports suggest that the number of circular migrants in India is up to 10 crores, contributing up to 10% to the national Gross Domestic Product (GDP). (Thorat and John, 2001) (NCEUS, 2008) (Deshingkar and Akter, 2009).

Emphasizing the shortcomings of the census data which does not adequately capture circular migration, Deshingkar and Akter (2009) argue that circular migration is the main form of mobility for work and that such migration is higher among the poor, especially scheduled castes (SCs) and scheduled tribes (STs). Referring to various field-based studies, they point out that the major subsectors that employ migrant labour are textiles, construction, stone quarries and mines, brick kilns, small-scale industries (diamond cutting, leather accessories etc.), crop transplanting and harvesting, sugarcane cutting, plantations, rickshaw pulling, food processing including fish and prawn processing, salt panning, domestic work, security services, sex work, small hotels and roadside restaurants/tea shops and street vending. (ibid) The construction sector, which is the highest contributor to the GDP in the non-farming sector, is one of the biggest employers of migrants. They compute the number of migrants working in the construction sector alone in India in the year 2008 to be around 40 million. (ibid)

The present study takes these insights from the emerging scholarship on migration to understand the work and life of Delhi's labour chowk workers. It approaches migration as a spectrum, varying from short term to long term, circulatory, and seasonal. The study focuses on workers who do not live in one residential area continuously for a long period of time. They move around different places looking for work, and some of them also go back to their villages seasonally. Some of them have managed to secure a foothold in the economy and a place to live in the city. The report attempts to explore the subjective experience of urban life from the narratives of the workers, who are placed on this spectrum of migration against the backdrop of the larger changes in the political economy, specifically the crisis in agrarian India that is forcing people to leave their villages and move to other places for survival.

3

Conversations From the Field Visits

The interviews were taken on the spot. Given the nature of their mobility, follow-up interviews were not possible in many cases. The intention here is not to factually ascertain the trends in migration, but to listen to workers and present a version of their life and understand how they make sense of their experiences. The following narratives speak about their lived reality, how they interpret mobility, spaces, and labour.

3.1.   On Love

Rajan Kumar and Sanjana[5]

Rajan Kumar Valmiki and his partner Sanjana Yadav have been on the run for the past few years. Their choice to work in the construction sector in Delhi NCR has a backstory of love. Rajan is from the district of Jhansi and Sanjana is from the district of Jalaun, both in UP. When we met them, they were about to share a few chapatis with each other for dinner.

'We have been starving since yesterday. Today, we met a thekedar we used to work with and asked him for Rs. 50. We bought these chapatis with that money.'

Like most of the migrant workers, they also carry a small gas stove attached with a cylinder wherever they go. If they do not find

---

5 Interview taken in October 2019

work for a few days and must stay and wait at the labour chowk, they cook on this stove. It is compact and is easy to carry wherever they travel for work. The couple was planning to sell it for some food before they met the thekedar.

Rajan owns 50 bighas of land back in his village. Because there is an acute shortage of water in the village and agriculture is no longer profitable, he had to lease out the land to someone else for an annual rent of Rs. 2,000 per bigha. When we asked him about the people who have migrated out of his village looking for work, he told us that most of the '*Harijans*' in his village migrate to the city for work. The Yadav community owns most of the land and cattle in the village, so they stay back. They are also the money lenders in his village. In addition to the income he receives from leasing out the land, Rajan also used to sell *gutka* (chewing tobacco) and cigarettes on a motorbike.

He was married to another woman before meeting Sanjana. His ex-wife had filed a complaint against him at the police station, and he was in police custody for a few days. After he was released, he moved to Jhansi and found work in a pay-and-use toilet. It was owned by a Thakur who would give him a share of the daily collection as his wage. It was during this time that he met Sanjana, who was on her way back from a pilgrimage. After using the toilet, she used Rajan's phone to call her husband. They had a small chat and she left for her village. They kept in touch with each other for months. 'She used to go to the terrace and talk whenever I rang her.' Sanjana could not stop giggling when he said this. When Rajan could not get through to her on the phone for several days, he decided to go to her village to see her. He knew that she was a Yadav and her husband a Verma. He befriended a tractor driver who showed him the settlement of the Vermas. He walked around their land until Sanjana saw him. They both decided to meet at a temple the next day. When they met at the temple, they decided to elope. 'I lied to my husband that I had a headache and took Rs. 13 with me when I left. I did not take anything else from that house,' said Sanjana. She had a 15-year-old son and a 14-year-old daughter when she decided to elope with Rajan. It was a lot of emotional turmoil for her, since she had to leave her family behind. She recalled, 'I did not know he was a Valmiki. I abused him a lot when I found out. I wouldn't have talked to him had I known that he belonged to a lower caste'.

When they took a bus to Jhansi from her village, Rajan did not know where to take her. They stayed inside the public toilet for two days. When someone from Sanjana's village found out that they were staying in Jhansi, her son and husband came to take her back. She hid under the toilet slab for a while, but they found her eventually. When her son reassured her that her husband would not beat her up, and begged her to return, she had no choice but to go back.

For several months, Sanjana stayed with her husband. But Rajan was persistent. He started making regular visits to her village. He used to wait for her outside her house to get her attention. She would pretend to go to the terrace to dry clothes just to see him from a distance. They were caught doing this by her son and husband, and Rajan was chased away from the village. Sanjana knew where Rajan's sister stayed, so one day, she lied to her family about going to the market to buy vegetables and reached his sister's house. They have been together ever since.

Both of them came to Delhi in search of work. Initially, a thekedar took them to a farm in Dehradun. The farm was the size of approximately 20 bighas and was owned by a colonel. Though they were hired as agricultural workers to grow cauliflowers, apart from farming, Sanjana also had to do the housework and Rajan had to run errands in the house. They worked there for three months, after which they left because the owner refused to pay them. They went back to Rajan's sister's house and set out for Delhi again with Rs. 5,000 that they had borrowed from Rajan's sister. Since then, they have been working at various construction sites in Delhi.

They had recently been spotted by one of Sanjana's relatives at their last workplace. A terrified Sanjana grabbed her valuables, and they both ran for their lives.

One of them saw me there, came up to me and said *Namaste*. The next day, they came on two motorbikes. I was sure that they were going to take me back home. So I ran with my belongings. I was wearing a green saree, and thankfully it matched with the colour of the bushes where I was hiding. They looked around and went back. We were scared to go back to that place and collect our wages.

Once again, Sanjana and Rajan ended up at the labour chowk with no money to buy food, and with no work.

3.2.   On Disability

Shivam Tyagi

It was under a flyover near the Shahdara labour chowk that we first met Shivam[6]. He was not alone. A couple of rickshaw pullers were taking a nap under the flyover, a middle-aged woman was boiling milk, and some were eating chapatis in a corner. Shivam had a bag full of medical documents which he kept under his head for support. He was being taken to the recovery shelter run by Hausla for medical assistance. When he was leaving, he held the medical certificate in one hand and a blanket in another. His friends were gathering around him to say goodbye. A well-dressed man who was walking through the road suddenly started shouting at one of the rickshaw pullers for tossing the newspaper in which his chapati was wrapped. 'These guys dirty this place so much,' he said, looking at us. Everybody quietly dispersed; Shivam sat in the auto. The next time we met him, he was watching a cricket match with others at the shelter. He was reluctant to leave the match and talk to us. Playing cricket was one of the things he missed while he was working in Delhi.

A young man of 24 years at the time of the interview, Shivam belongs to Hapur village in Meerut district, Uttar Pradesh. His mother died young and his father remarried when Shivam was a child. His father had two more children from his second marriage and then passed away. Thereafter, Shivam was raised by his step-

____

6   Interview taken in July 2017

mother, who had her own two very young children to care for. She worked as an agricultural labourer and took care of Shivam till he was 13 years old. Shivam describes his childhood as difficult. He received little attention from his stepmother while growing up. Though there was a school in their village, she did not have the means to send him to school.

He still remembers the day he reached Delhi. He took a train and reached Shahdara station. He wandered around for a bit and fell asleep on the platform. When he woke up the next morning, he saw a couple of workers walking towards the labour chowk and decided to follow them to the chowk. A *rajmistri* (chief mason) took him to a construction site as a helper.

He was paid Rs. 150 that day. Hungry and tired, he went to a dhaba and ate a lot of food with some of the money he had made. He kept the rest of it in his pocket and went back to the railway platform to sleep. The next morning, he woke up to realize his money had been stolen. He went back to the labour chowk again. Someone who later became his friend took him along to work as a headload worker and paid him Rs. 400 for four hours of work. That is when he realized that working as a headload worker is better paid than construction work. To befriend him, he began to get this person *gutka*, and their friendship eventually grew.

According to Shivam, usually workers at the labour chowk keep a distance from one another. But when his friend asked him to move in with him, that was a big gesture of friendship for Shivam. From the platform, he moved into a rented room with others. The Rs. 3,000 rent was shared equally between them. Finding work also became easier for all of them as they would call and inform one another when they found contractors at the chowk. They started getting work regularly.

However, they had to move out of the room within a few days because of an untoward incident. Most of Shivam's friends used to get drunk after work. Sometimes, when the contractor was happy with the workers, he would throw a party for them. One of his roommates was an alcoholic who, in the throes of his intoxication, picked a fight with the owner of the house. They were asked to vacate that place, after which they moved to a new place, leaving the alcoholic roommate to fend for himself. They bought utensils and a gas cylinder to cook. Since Shivam used to cook for all of them, he did not have to pay for the groceries. After six months, they moved to a cheaper place in Loni, a place on the border of Uttar Pradesh and Delhi. The rent was Rs. 1,500, split equally by three of them.

All the roommates started to commute to the labour chowk every day from their room. By then, Shivam had become skilled at handling heavy goods. He then came to know about 'chain kuppi' (chain pulley). It involves carrying heavy goods using a crane and moving the crane and other machinery manually. It would take 2-3 hours each day, and the pay was higher than construction work. When Shivam started to move away from construction work to chain kuppi, there was a period of stability in his life. He managed to save around Rs. 1,45,000. He moved into a rented room by himself and made friends at work. He became close to a person named Raju with whom he started to drink occasionally. Eventually, he started visiting Raju's room regularly, where he would drink with Raju and his girlfriend. One day, when all three of them were drunk, Shivam expressed his interest to get married to the girlfriend's sister. The only thing he knew about her was that she was from Bengal. They asked him to come back to their house when sober, so he went the next day after work. Raju's girlfriend asked him about his family and income. They tried to reject his proposal by saying that the room he lived in was not good enough to start a family. Shivam promised that he would move to a better room, or even move back to his house in the village if necessary. He was in love. When he got work in Goa, they would go to Goa together.

But things started getting a little sinister when Raju demanded money from Shivam. Initially, he asked to borrow Rs. 5,000, but later asked Shivam to arrange money for the wedding. According to Shivam, once Raju had taken all his savings, he started delaying the wedding. A year passed by. It was around the time of Chhat Puja that the talks around the wedding resurfaced. Raju asked Shivam to accompany him to Bengal so that the marriage ceremony could be conducted in the girl's village. However, on the day they were supposed to leave for Bengal, Shivam was told of a change of plans and asked to stay back in Delhi. Shivam waited for months, but no one returned.

Having lost all his savings by then, Shivam had to work very hard in the coming days. He found different kinds of work which could fetch him more money within fewer working hours. He was engaged to carry Malaysian wood from trucks, where he was paid around Rs. 5,000–6,000 for shifting an entire truckful of wood. This money was divided among 5-6 workers the contractor had picked up from the labour chowk. Additionally, he also worked with what he described as '*Avo light ka kaam*'. This work involved fixing fancy lights for stage shows based in Rithala. He enjoyed it because he got to see celebrities at these shows. For an entire event, which sometimes lasted for three nights, he was paid Rs. 1,800. During this period, Shivam worked as a headload worker during the day, and worked the stage shows at night.

The work schedule was hectic, but Shivam wanted to save money and go back to his village. One day after three consecutive nights without sleep, he finally went back to his room to sleep and suddenly, the power went off. It was summer and the room was very hot. Frustrated and tired, he went up to the terrace to get some sleep. That night changed his life. The terrace of his building did not have walls; he fell down from the third floor when he was asleep. His friends immediately took him to GTB Hospital. He was screaming in pain, but the doctors refused to treat him, asking his friends to take him to the government hospital in Safdarjung instead.

At Safdarjung Hospital, they informed him that the treatment would cost around Rs. 30,000. For Shivam, that was a huge amount to manage within such a short period of time. He had managed to save just Rs. 10,000 from all the sleepless nights he spent working.

The only choice for him then was to return to his room. Climbing up the stairs to reach his room was in itself a hellish task for Shivam. The toilets on the ground floor were inaccessible. He could not get up to fetch himself food. He was dependent on his friends even to be able to turn around in sleep. His friends were also dependent on the labour chowks for work, and so Shivam could not bother them for very long. The only place to which he could think of moving was the flyover near Shahdara station. His priority was an accessible toilet, so chose a spot which was close to it. He was also familiar with the people around the station since the labour chowk was close by. The flower seller would safekeep his savings for him. He was also friends with the caretaker of the toilet. A woman who shared the space under the flyover with him cooked for him, and the security guard of the ATM also brought him food when he was hungry. He did not care about the flies or the dirt; being able to access a toilet was more important to him than anything else.

When we met Shivam for the first time, it had been 40 days since the accident. Someone had stolen the bag that had his clothes. He was broke and completely dependent on the familiar people around for food. After going to the shelter, he had surgery and could walk without the help of others. He wishes to go back to work but is unsure if he would be able to carry heavy goods as he used to.

3.3. On Debt

Chunnilal and family[7]

We met a family of eight from Mirchwara village in Lalitpur, Uttar Pradesh. Pramod and Chunnilal are brothers who came here with their wives and children, and a distant relative. They have three more brothers. The eldest one had migrated to Indore to find work in the construction industry, while the younger brothers stayed back at home with their aged parents. Chunnilal has been coming to the chowk for the past 11 years. In the earlier days, the spot

---

7   Interview taken in October 2019

where they wait for work was a little further away from the present place, and it was called Nizamuddin Chowk instead of Sarai Kale Khan chowk. His wife and brother have been coming with him to the Sarai Kale Khan labour chowk for a few years now. The brother's wife, however, is fairly new to the city.

They belong to the Prajapati/Kumhar caste of Madhya Pradesh whose traditional occupation is pottery. Thakurs, Kurmis, and Yadavs are the land-owning castes in their village. The rest of the castes (Ahirwars, Kushwahas, Dhimars, Kadayyas and Kumhars) migrate to different parts of India for work. Some of the Kushwahas also own land. According to Chunnilal, the Dhimars (traditionally boatmen) were the first to lose their livelihood and migrate. They do not own land. Kumhars, a scheduled caste, also own very little land. Thakurs, the biggest landowners, lease out their land to other 'lower' castes. Like many others, their village has been facing acute drought for the past few years. Since most farmers are tenants of the land-owning castes, the benefits of the drought packages are received largely by the Thakurs and other upper castes. According to the family, the extinction of traditional occupations, landlessness, and drought forced two-thirds of their village to migrate to the cities.

Their father was a potter. He used to collect clay from the riverside, mould it and make pottery wares for a living. When the brothers were younger, the pottery trade and the yield from the three bigha land they shared with their father's family, was sufficient for survival. However, the father developed a neurological disorder and stopped making earthenware. None of the siblings had learnt the craft because it needs more effort than daily wage work. The clay has to be collected and carried to their houses, mixed proportionately and once the pots are moulded, they are baked in a kiln to firm them. The last stage is risky; the success rate is usually 50-50 because the vessel may break due to over/under heating. No one except their *chacha* (uncle) does this work in the family anymore. Prior to moving to Delhi for construction work, the siblings were involved in casual stone mining work in their village. The stones are mined from the common land in the village and are used to build houses. Chunnilal, the eldest of the brothers, had blisters all over his palms because of this work. According to his wife, the work they did in the village used to fetch them Rs. 150–200 a day.

When we asked whether they were beneficiaries of any state programs or schemes, the couple told us that they were also doing MGNREGA work in their village. Even though they finished 90 days of work, they had only received the wages for 45 days thus far. The wages get credited directly in their account.

They came to Delhi for the first time along with their three children two months before the interview. Their eldest child is nine years old and goes to school, so they left her in an uncle's care back in the village. When they first arrived, they got work immediately at a construction site near the Gurgaon Bus Stand. They thought that they would not have to wait at all this time around either. However, when we met with the family, which was around midnight, they had been waiting all day, having been unable to find a thekedar as it was raining. The jhuggi, which the thekedar had provided to them, was relatively more comfortable for them than sleeping in the street.

Chunnilal's wife cooks for the entire family and also works at the construction site. Like all other women, her day starts at 5 AM. She has to cook for the family, wash clothes, clean utensils, feed her children, before she leaves for work at 8 AM. She was four months pregnant at the time of the interview. She had miscarried a few months prior when something fell on her head after she fell down at the construction site. They went to the nearby hospitals and enquired about whether they could demand compensation some way.

The jhuggi that the contractor had arranged for them did not have an electricity supply or gas connection. They get a kerosene lantern to use at night. Food is cooked on the *chulha* (stove). They get subsidized food grains from the ration shop back home. The shopkeeper is particularly helpful in their village: if they cannot collect the ration in the same month, they are allowed to collect it the next month. The family carries their allotted food grains and some essential utensils to the city when they migrate. It takes 12 hours by train to reach Nizamuddin Railway Station. They travel with cooked food that can last them the day or two they might have to wait for the thekedar. As they get paid only after working for a particular period, the grains and spices they carry from their village ensure their food security for the first few days at work.

The wages for men and women are unequal in practice. Even though Chunnilal and his wife are aware of their right to be paid equally, they do not want to sabotage their livelihood by asking for higher wages. 'My wife works more than me. Even then, she gets paid Rs. 250 a day and I get 300. We need to survive somehow, so we have learned to be happy with whatever little we get.'

They have to take days off work if they fall ill at the site. Chunnilal's brother had a fever for a few days. His wife, who is also a worker, had to stay back to take care of him. A resident near their worksite directed him to a government hospital in Gurgaon, where he got a consultation with the doctor for free.

The debt crisis that their entire region goes through was evident from their experience. Each adult member of the family has a loan of at least Rs. 40,000 on them, which they borrowed at a monthly interest rate of five percent. Chunnilal himself pays Rs. 2,600 just as interest every month on the loan he has taken. When he has to pay back the loan, he borrows money from someone else. This is more or less the way every migrant worker from his village manages their debt. When we asked him whether he has to furnish any land documents against the loan, he told us he does not have any in his name. The lack of ownership of property is one reason why they mostly rely on informal money lenders.

Other than NREGA, the only welfare scheme he has been able to avail is the Ujjwala Yojna, through which they received a gas stove and gas cylinders. Since the *sarpanch* is a Thakur, most of the schemes do not reach them, as Chunnilal's wife explains, because of the prevailing caste biases in accessing government schemes.

When we asked them about their plans to go back, they said they will when it starts raining in their village, as people will resume agricultural work once water is available.

3.4. On Caste and Land

Dhaniram Kushwaha[8]

We met Dhaniram Kushwaha at the Sarai Kale Khan labour chowk. Many of the workers we met there listed *chakbandi* (land consolidation) as one of the reasons for them having to migrate. To understand the act and the process more deeply, we decided to visit Dhaniram's village in Lalitpur. The Uttar Pradesh Consolidation of Holdings Act (1952), and The Uttar Pradesh Consolidation of Holdings (Amendment) Act (1970), known as the Uttar Pradesh Chakbandi Act, were enacted to ensure the consolidation of agricultural holdings for the development of agriculture. According to these laws, a committee has to be formed with the agreement of the Gram Sabha to proceed with the *chakbandi* in any region. As per Dhaniram and many others from the Kushwaha community, this process is nothing but an exercise through which the land-owning caste accumulates the most productive land in a village.

The *chakbandi* in Narahat village was initiated a few years ago. A majority of the villagers, who belong to different OBC and Scheduled Caste communities, were unaware of the actual consequences of the process of land consolidation when it began. Kushwahas, a caste traditionally engaged in agriculture, form half of the population in the village. However, according to Dhaniram, Sahus and Thakurs, who are the minority in the village, own almost half of the land. Dhaniram's father, a Kushwaha, had owned 10 acres of land, which was to be divided among two of his sons. Similarly, most of the Kushwaha people own land of size between 2–15 acres, depending on the size of the family. There are a few land-owning families from the Chamar (SC) community in the area; the rest of

---

8   Interview taken in October 2019

the landless families belong to OBC and SC communities. They are entitled to receive land after the land consolidation, wherein 10% of the surveyed land is supposed to be kept aside to redistribute among the landless, and to be used for common needs of the village. This land-caste nexus, however, forms the foundation for an extremely corrupt process where the agricultural land of small farmers gets further fragmented while the land of the rich farmers gets consolidated for their convenience.

Dhaniram's family jointly owned 10 acres of land which, after the *chakbandi*, was reduced to one acre. Instead of consolidating the land, the officials have further fragmented it into 20 parts. According to the guidelines, if there are trees, wells, etc. on a part of the land, the consolidation is to be focused around this piece of land. Dhaniram, on the other hand, lost around 15 trees to a Thakur after the *chakbandi*. The most productive land went to the Thakurs and Brahmins in the village. While *chakbandi* is the legal means through which the dominant castes acquired land, the oppressed castes have been losing their land in different ways. When one of the Thakurs started encroaching on his land for cultivation, Dhaniram was told: 'You can go and work outside the village and earn wages, we can't. We only know how to farm, so why don't you let us do it!'

In another instance, another Kushwaha in the village had bought a water pump for his small plot of land. This is pertinent because the groundwater in Bundelkhand region is lower than the normal level, and it is almost unaffordable for the small farmers to dig a well and get water throughout the year. Rivers and streams are the primary source of water in this region. The pump set he got was smashed by a Thakur because he did not wait for his turn to pump water. 'The Thakurs and Brahmins get to pump the water first, followed by the Kushwahas and Ahariyas,' said Dhaniram. That pump set, once worth thousands of rupees and now lying broken in his courtyard, is a testament to the violence of continuing caste oppression and the politics of land use. Similarly, the upper castes occupy even public roads and pavements in the village to grow their crops. As a result, people who do not have direct access to the roads are forced to wait till the Thakurs harvest the illegally grabbed public land and vacate it, to transport their own harvest.

According to the villagers of Budki Khera in Bundelkhand, where Dhaniram's relatives live, 80% of the Dalits and Adivasis migrate to Delhi and Bhopal to work in the brick kiln industry or the construction sector. In the case of the Lodhis, the dominant caste of the village, only the poorest 10% migrate. The village has one Jain family which is the largest landowner. It is not a coincidence that the Pradhan of the village also happens to be a Jain.

From Dhaniram's family, everyone except the old mother and the school-going children migrated to Delhi for construction work. The opportunities for work available to them are limited. People who do not migrate to Delhi work in the village quarry for a meagre wage of Rs. 150 a day and a pouch of cheap alcohol. The opportunities for construction work in the village are also limited, and even if they find work, they are only paid Rs. 100–200 a day. On the other hand, the wages are almost twice as much in cities like Delhi, so people who have contacts there migrate to different cities. According to Dhaniram's wife, mothers mostly migrate with their babies and pregnant women work till the month of delivery.

We met another family in Budki Khera, Tikamgarh District, which shared similar stories about caste, land, and migration. When we visited Radha's house, she gathered all the men in her extended family who migrate to Delhi for construction work. They were all from the Aherwar community, a Scheduled Caste. They told us that though their traditional occupation was cattle skinning, it had long been abandoned and they were now agricultural workers in the fields of land-owning Lodhis.

For the Ahirwars, the opportunities in the construction industry outside have been a way to escape unpaid labour under the upper castes. Rahul, a second-generation migrant worker from their village said:

> 'Earlier, they would just ask our parents to go and work in their field. The wage is food, that was the rule. I am 23 years old now, but this was the practice even when I started working. Right now, since we go to the cities for work, we demand wages for our work in the harvesting seasons here also.'

According to a group of young Ahirwar men we spoke to, the migration started 20–25 years ago. They also said that the single men mostly go to labour chowks, while some of the women who migrate with their husbands and children prefer to work with fixed thekedars in construction projects. According to them, the arrangement with the thekedars ensures work for a fixed amount of time along with a place to stay within the premises of the construction projects. Women prefer this arrangement because, in certain cases, they can contribute a small share of money to compensate for the wage of a female worker who takes care of the children when the mothers are away for work. Women who are not looking to work for a longer period of time choose to go to the labour chowk. The payments from the builders are made at the end of each week.

Unfortunately, fraudulence by the thekedars is a common occurrence. Everyone we spoke to complained about how the thekedars ran away with their money. For some, it is a day's wage or two, while for others it is up to a month's wage.

Most of the land in the Budki Khera village is owned by Lodhis, who are in numerical majority; four Brahmin families, and a Jain family. Jains and Lodhis are also money lenders and nearly all of the Ahirwar families have borrowed money from them against their land. Ahirwars, Gaikwads, and Sors, who constitute a considerable proportion of the population in the village, are politically under-represented too. Historically, the village has had only one Pradhan from the Dalit community, and that was Radha's father. According to her, when he decided to contest for re-election, her father was threatened by the upper-caste goons and forced to back out.

According to the local activists we met there, the groundwater level is too low and the farmers who can't afford to dig a borewell or afford a pump set are dependent solely on the rain for irrigation. They grew *urad dal* (black gram lentils) but it was all soaked in the rain, adding to their misery. On the other hand, many abandoned the two-season (*Rabi and Kharif*) farming system and sowed only one seasonal crop after the continuous occurrence of drought. Our visits were in the peak monsoons and on our way to the villages, we passed by many ponds and dams. While big landowners manage to draw water through borewells and pumps, the small farmers are not able to afford this infrastructure to support their agriculture. Most of them told us that it is futile to invest in the small patches of land since they are completely scattered.

During the drought, compensation for the losses incurred by these small and marginal farmers is mostly claimed by the upper castes because of their political influence. Each family that migrates to the city owes the Lodhis anywhere from Rs. 2,000 to Rs. 2,00,000, which they borrow at an interest rate of 4–5% per month against their land. If they are not able to pay back their debt, the land is seized by the upper-caste lender. Almost all of them said that the money earned from construction is mostly used to pay back this debt, borrowed mainly for family emergencies or weddings.

Nibhar[9]

We met Nibhar at Rampul (labour) chowk near Lajpat Nagar, Delhi. He was one of the oldest workers we met there. He has been working as a painter for the past 40 years and regularly comes to the chowk for work even at the age of 60. He was pleased to find an audience to share some of his political criticisms of the current government and their inaction. He introduced himself as a 'Harijan' from Gonda district, Uttar Pradesh.

---

9   Interview taken in October 2017

Nibhar's family consists of seven daughters and a wife, to whom he was married at the age of five. 'Things were different in the village; my father went and saw my wife and fixed the match. I met her for the first time when I was 17, though,' he laughed. Though Nibhar has a small plot of land back in his village, when the family grew bigger, he had no choice but to move to Delhi.

He described the changes which have taken place at the chowk ever since he came there at the age of 20. The place where the chowk is located now used to be a working-class *basti* called Gandhi Camp Jhuggi. In Nibhar's memory, the buildings back then were really small. He lived in a jhuggi in the *basti* for 15 years. Pointing to an empty plot behind us, he described a different landscape he was familiar with:

> Look at that plot, almost 10,000–12,000 people used to live there. All these houses around here were really small; some of them have now built another floor above the ground floor, and all the other houses were built almost 20–25 years ago.

Nibhar and other workers have built the colony around them together with their own hands, but they could never afford a house there themselves. Once the construction was over and the class composition in the neighbourhood changed, the government evicted the workers' settlement. Earlier, the workers used to wait outside their jhuggis for work. They continued to visit this space since they had built contacts with the agents and contractors. The place eventually turned into a labour chowk. But once the settlement was demolished, most of them did not have a place to live. Some people who were able to provide documented proof of residence were resettled in Holambi colony. Many like Nibhar did not have proof of residence. In his own words:

> People told me I will have to produce a ration card to get the house. The Pradhan and the other leaders would take Rs. 5,000–10,000 in bribes. I did not have enough money to bribe them. I had seven young daughters to look after, you know?

After the eviction, he once again moved to another *basti* near Ashram. Many of his friends went back to the village. Like most of the people who come to the chowk from his village, Nibhar's income from wage labour offsets the expenses associated with the cost of agriculture in the village.

> We all are farmers. There is not enough work back in the village. Even if we work there, we get Rs. 200 per day. Household expenses such as buying oil, buying turmeric powder, buying fertilizers, all these things are managed with the money I get from here. Prices are going up for everything. Even tea leaves cost a lot these days. It will soon come to around Rs. 250 a day. How can I manage it? I manage by working as a farmer and also working as a painter.

When he is away, his wife and children work on the farm. The demand for painting work goes down in winters and monsoon, so Nibhar goes back home and joins them in these months.

Although he sends all his daughters to school, he is critical of the government schools in their village. 'I am sending my all daughters to school. One of them is in seventh standard. I was travelling with her on a train and asked her to read a poster. She could not read it. What are they taught in school, I wonder!' He wants to send his children to private schools, but with this income, he hardly manages their daily needs. Because he stays alone in Delhi, he cuts corners on his own food. Dal-roti is a rare meal; he usually has to manage with roti and salt, or roti and chutney, which he makes in his room.

In his opinion, along with the real wages being lower when he started working, prices have also increased over time. He illustrates the impact of inflation on the workers through an example:

> 'When I came first here, I used to earn Rs. 5 a day. I would buy rations—dal, rice, oil, masalas, and everything I needed in a month— with Rs. 15. Now I buy monthly rations for Rs. 1,500. I eat my roti with a chutney or just salt towards the end of the month. The daily wage has increased but so have the prices. Now you can imagine how poor people like us survive.'

The wages he gets from paint work fluctuate depending on the availability of work. When he is out of work, he settles for a rate as low as Rs. 350 per day; the standard rate is Rs. 600. When he does not have enough money to send home, his wife borrows from relatives. However, they did not take any loans from the government.

He was particularly critical of the lack of land reforms in UP. The land he owns was distributed to them in Prime Minister Indira Gandhi's tenure, Nibhar explained. He admired Indira Gandhi's efforts to take away land from the landowners and distribute it to the poor. According to him, the *zamindars* back in his village create a ruckus for them even today, and many of the villagers once took this issue to the government. He tried to meet many political leaders, including Narendra Modi, to demand further land reform. A concrete solution for the problems of the poor, according to him, lies in implementing land ceiling and redistributing the land amongst the poor.

3.5.   On Homelessness and Gender

Interview with Meena and Sheela[10]

When we reached the Sarai Kale Khan labour chowk at 9:30 PM, most of the people were awake. There were about a hundred people in the street, looking for a comfortable corner in which to sleep. Families and neighbours usually stay together, while the spaces under the flyover are claimed by the usual residents of the street: rickshaw pullers, beggars, the disabled and the destitute, etc. The divider that separates the road to Nizamuddin station and the footpath along the turn is where migrants mostly wait for work and sleep. There are also two shelter homes on this road. Migrant workers, however, rarely use this facility.

When we met Meena and Sheela's family, the kids were falling asleep on their lap. They took out the *chatai* (bamboo rug) and laid

---

10 Interview taken in July 2018

it down for the kids to sleep on. Sheela was three months pregnant at the time of the interview; Meena had three children: a toddler, a girl, and a boy. They were sisters-in-law and had come to Delhi with their husbands and children, looking for work. They are originally from Badagaon in the Tikamgarh district of Madhya Pradesh, which is one of the many drought-affected districts of the Bundelkhand region. Meena has been working in the construction sector for the past 20 years, even before her son, who is now in his late teens, was born. Her husband used to be a dancer; they belong to a community which is, as part of their traditional occupation, mainly invited to dance at weddings. Sheela was relatively new to the chowk; she got married to Meena's husband's brother some years back and joined him when he was coming to Delhi. Meena and her husband had 5 bighas of land back in their village, which, according to them, they had received from the government during Chief Minister Mayawati's tenure. They come to Delhi for two to four months and go back to their village for the harvest season.

All of them gathered around us when we went to meet them. The family explained why a lot of people from the same region are present at the labour chowk. Agriculture is seasonal in their village. The month of *Kaatak* (as per the lunar calendar; also known as Kartik—this is the harvest season for monsoon crops) is for *gehu* (wheat), soybean, *urad* (black gram), and *arhar* (red gram). In their opinion, the lack of rainfall has affected the cultivation of wheat in the entire region. The main source of income in their village is the Mahua tree from which country liquor is brewed. Earlier, they would sell the home-grown wheat in the market, but now they mostly grow it for subsistence. They also grow vegetables but not to sell them. The market rate for wheat in their village is Rs. 20–25 per kilogram, and Rs. 30–40 per kilogram for Mahua flowers. However, when they sell it, they get less than half the price as the middlemen take a huge cut.

When the family prepares for the journey to Delhi, they pack the home-grown *dal, besan* (chickpea flour), *atta* (whole wheat flour) and the few vegetables that keep for longer. The food supplies they get from home are sufficient for almost a month, till they get their wages from the thekedar who hires them for construction sites.

According to Meena and Sheela, almost half of their village migrates to Delhi during certain seasons. There are approximately 400 households in the village. The duration and the frequency of their stay are determined by the amount of the land they have back at home, and the seasonal requirements of labour for agricultural work. According to them, caste groups such as Teli, Thakur, Brahmin, and Eka do not migrate. Paid work is available only for about as long as a month's time back in their village, though this already-scarce employment is also drying up as a result of the drought. The intensity of the drought was explained in the following words: 'Earlier we were expected to give only silver (as dowry) in weddings, these days we are expected to give gold.'

They clarified that this does not mean that there was no starvation or hunger earlier. When there wasn't enough to eat, they would turn to a food grain called *kodo*, but people are now embarrassed to eat it anymore. On probing further, they explained that *kodo* is a weed that grows in uncultivated fields.

None of them have received any assistance from the government, monetary or otherwise, to help them cope with the crisis. When we asked them whether the government has ever intervened, they said that though it has set up pension schemes in the Bundelkhand region, it never reaches them, according to Meena.

While we were talking, Meena's husband suddenly started singing for us a Bhojpuri tune that he improvised on by adding 'Madam' to the song's character. He had a long wig that he carried along with his essential things. His daughter also started dancing with him after a while, but the elder son was quite annoyed by this. Meena later explained that the son was embarrassed of his father's habit of dancing. Her father-in-law also did not like his son dancing and had asked him to stop his practice. She explained that the dance form is called *Ravala,* where men dress up and act as women. Each performance would fetch them Rs. 500 a day, but it was not a stable source of income for their family.

While they are satisfied with the facilities which they get at the worksite, which includes a jhuggi arranged by the thekedar, water, and electricity, they find waiting for work at the chowk the most unbearable part of their journey. Meena said:

> I haven't taken a bath for two days now. We have to pay Rs. 10 to use the public bathroom, and the children often get very frustrated with the heat and the noise, so I would rather get a packet of biscuits for my children with that money, that would calm them down for 3-4 hours.

Sheela, on the other hand, has her own troubles. The strenuous work, along with the pregnancy, gives her a backache. She has access to the Anganwadi (rural childcare centre) and the health workers at the worksite. The Anganwadi worker had once taken her to the hospital for a check-up and ultrasound. The dates usually given by the government hospitals are too far from the required date, so she had to spend Rs. 1,500 for getting tested in a private hospital.

When Meena came here first, which was 20 years ago, she was paid Rs. 50-60 for a day's work. Now, the unskilled male and female workers gets Rs. 350 a day, while the skilled workers get Rs. 500 a day. Her day at the worksite starts at 4 AM: she cleans the utensils, cooks for the children, washes the clothes, and gets ready for work. Her youngest daughter is looked after by her daughter who is a few years older. They get a lunch break at 1 PM, which is when she comes back to the jhuggi to get food for her husband, the children, and herself. Once the lunch break is over, she continues to work until 6 PM. After coming back home, she cooks for the entire family again and then finally gets to sleep. Childcare is not a big burden for her, since her older children help her out with the infant. Both of them are enrolled in a school back in their village.

At work, she has to mix the cement mixture (which is locally referred to as *masala*) and carry it to different floors in the building. She also sweeps the floor to clear it of rubble before she leaves the worksite. The thekedar either takes them to the workplace in his own vehicle or pays them to hire a vehicle. They are happy with the work they get from the thekedar. They told us that they have never had a bad experience with the thekedar. 'When we are at the village, we long to be in the city; when we are here, we want to go back home,' Sheela said. The entire family sometimes manages to find work together. But if they do not, the brothers and their families meet back in the village after some time.

When they fall sick, they leave the city immediately and go back to their village. They do not trust the doctors in the city. (According to Satyaveerji, that is because the doctors in the village prescribe high-dose medicines).

They like this labour chowk because there is enough space for everyone to sleep peacefully. However, they feel that when there are more people, they are forced to sleep on rough surfaces such as the pavement near the shelter.

3.6.   On Drought and Migration

Guddi[11]

Guddi is a regular at the Sarai Kale Khan labour chowk. Most of the trains from Madhya Pradesh come to the Hazrat Nizamuddin Railway Station, so it was convenient for her to go to the labour chowk nearby to find work. She told us that initially, it was quite difficult for her to navigate this space. She had arrived with her husband and child, and found the labour chowk so crowded that they could not understand what to do. They walked around nearby to find a comfortable place to sleep. They decided on a parking lot near the pay-and-use toilet in the area. When they were half asleep, the police came and drove them away from there. Eventually, they found out that the police allow the workers to sleep only in the more public part of the street. This time around, she had come

---

11   Interview taken in July 2018

to the labour chowk with her youngest child, husband, brother-in-law, and a cousin. Her husband is more familiar with Delhi. When we met Guddi, her husband had gone to speak to the thekedar.

The family comes from a village close to Jabalpur, named Chirola. When we asked her if she owned any land, Guddi responded by saying that only the Chouhans and Thakurs in her village own land. The couple used to work as labourers on a farm that grew *chana* (gram) and soybean. Guddi's wage was Rs. 150 a day, while her husband would get Rs. 250 for a day's work. Conditions of acute drought have affected the agricultural practices in the region, so they had no option but to migrate to Delhi for construction work. Guddi's natal family owns five acres of land back in their village Damoli. However, as a married daughter of the family, she has not been given any right to inheritance over the land. The Damoli region is comparatively more fertile than her husband's place. 'If we are labourers, we have to migrate,' Guddi said, when asked why the family chose to migrate. The government did not compensate anyone for the drought in their village. Even if they did, as mere workers on the farm they would not have received any compensation. The only welfare scheme they avail from the government is the public distribution system for rations. They do not know of the implementation status of the MNREGA in the village.

The family came to the Sarai Kale Khan Labour chowk a few months ago in the monsoons. The thekedar gave them an advance of Rs. 1,000 for food and other daily needs, and they live in the jhuggis provided at the worksite. There is no guarantee that the thekedar will provide electricity at the jhuggi. They have to buy firewood from outside to set up the firewood oven.

Guddi has four children. The eldest one is studying in the 10th standard, and the younger ones are in 9th, 8th and in 3rd respectively. When she came to Delhi the last time, she left all the children back in the village. However, when she went back, she realized that the youngest one found it particularly difficult to live without her. Hence, this time she brought the youngest child along.

When we asked her about her daily schedule at the workplace, she mentioned that the timings change according to the facilities they receive. Sometimes she has to collect firewood after work, and in some places, there is a long wait for water as the queue is long. Usually, she wakes up at five in the morning and goes to work by eight. In these three hours, she cooks for the entire family, cleans the utensils, and then washes the clothes. If the jhuggi is close to the worksite, they all come back home to eat; if it is far, they carry packed food to the worksite. Guddi comes back at 6 PM and then does housework, which mainly involves cooking and cleaning. She eats after she is done serving her family their dinner, and then goes off to sleep.

We met her on the second day of the couple's arrival at the chowk for this season. They had been unable to find a suitable thekedar in those two days. They think there simply isn't enough work. When we asked them how they eat when they don't get work, they said that they eat '*sardarji ka khana,*' referring to the *langar* (communal meals) served at the Gurudwara nearby.

When we were talking to Guddi, a family sitting close by joined the conversation. Raju, his wife, their uncle, and their child arrived at the labour chowk the previous day in the same train as Guddi and had been waiting for work since then. Even though they had worked in construction earlier, this was the first time they had come to Delhi looking for work. The couple have three children. The eldest is studying in the 8th standard, while the other two are in seventh and first standard respectively. The eldest son had accompanied them to the labour chowk. When we asked them about what would happen to his education, Raju responded by saying: '*Paisa nahi hai toh kaise school bhejega?*' (If we do not earn money, how do we send them to school?). When asked if their income from construction work would be sufficient to send the children to school, their immediate response was that their survival is the priority before education. They also referred to *chakbandi* (land consolidation reforms) as a decisive factor in their village that had fragmented their land. The family had one bigha land, which was divided into 20 parts after the *chakbandi*. They shared a similar story about land fragmentation, where the upper-caste communities had managed to grab the most fertile land. Because the process is underway, they cannot work on their own land (as it may go to someone else), so all of them had to come to Delhi for survival. Raju is from the Kushwaha caste, which comes under the OBCs (Other Backward Classes). According to him, the revenue official is from the Chamar caste (SC) and is incompetent as he is not redistributing the land at all. To clarify his statement, we further probed him on whether people from the Chamar caste own most land anyway—what was the reason the official was not fulfilling his responsibilities? He said that even though they don't own land, the landlords are from the Thakur caste, and ultimately, they make the decisions. Raju's family does not own a pump set or an *indara*,[12] and is hence dependent solely on the rains for irrigation and other use on the farm. Otherwise, they use water from a common borewell for their daily needs. They grow corn, wheat, soybean, groundnuts etc, if the weather is favourable. When agriculture was more sustainable, they used to earn around Rs. 12,000 a month, and to supplement this, they would take up other daily wage work within the village itself. The daily wage income, combined with the income from agriculture, was sufficient to run the household. According to them, people are increasingly migrating out of their village due to the lack of water in their farms. They were a bit cautious about coming to Delhi because their neighbours, who came before them, reported not being paid wages for four out of the six months they spent working for a thekedar. However, Raju and his family were hopeful that they would find a better thekedar and a jhuggi to live in at the construction site itself. Whether or not the women would migrate was a decision that was based not on safety or the amenities available for them, but on whether there was cattle and

---

12 Indara is a colloquial name for a well because they were dug widely during Prime Minister Indira Gandhi's tenure.

land to take care of back home. They told us that sometimes the entire family migrates to the city, and sometimes the women have to stay back to take care of the elders, the cattle, and their farmland.

3.7. On Low Wages and Long Working Hours

Ashok[13]

Ashok was quiet when we asked him about his home. He mentioned that he had left his wife and did not want to get into the details. He has been working at hotels and dhabas as a waiter and as a multi-tasker in wedding parties over the years. He is from the Kori caste of Meerut, Uttar Pradesh. Back in his city, most of the land is owned by Thakur and Rajwadi castes, while Gujjars, Tyagis, and Jats have medium-sized landholdings. He brought up the same caste names when we asked him about working conditions in the dhabas. Gujjars and Jats own most of the dhabas in Haryana; Ashok has witnessed many instances where the owners keep the workers captive:

> If you are willing to work for a longer time, you would get paid at the end of the term. If you want to leave before that, it's not just that you won't get any money, they will break your arms and legs, and lock you up in a room.

He spoke casually about the trauma of this captivity. He recalls that one of his co-workers was beaten up right in front of him for wanting to leave. When we asked him if the brokers or the police at the chowk take any responsibility for such torture, he replied, 'they are only bothered about their own cut, nobody cares if poor people are starving.'

Ashok travelled to different towns in Haryana, Rajasthan, and Ghaziabad in Uttar Pradesh before coming to Delhi. It was the acute unemployment in his city that forced him to migrate to different cities in search of work and take up different jobs. He has studied till the sixth standard and his brother has pursued higher education. His brother aspired to secure a government job but was

---

13 Interview taken in March 2019

unable to. Both of them are working as wage labourers now. Ashok first moved to Ghaziabad as a headload worker. When we asked him why he decided to move to Delhi, he laughed and said: '*Dilli hai dilwalon ki*' (Delhi is a city of big-hearted people). He came to know about shaadi-party (wedding party) work in Delhi when he was working as a headload worker in Ghaziabad. However, after reaching Delhi, he could not find such work immediately. He was barely earning enough to be able to eat.

> 'There were days when I earned a little more than required, I would go to a hotel to eat on those days. We cannot always be dependent on Hanuman Mandir and Gurudwara, right?'.

Like many other homeless people, paying for his own food was a luxury to Ashok. They rely mainly on the free food provided by Gurudwaras and a temple near Yamuna Pushta, where most of the shelters are located. During the initial months, he worked as a cart puller and a headload worker. He mostly lived on the streets until he moved to the shelter home run by Aman Biradari five years ago. When he moved there, he met other workers at the shelter who went to Company Baug.

According to Ashok, people from Company Baug mostly work in line hotels—small and medium sized roadside eateries are referred to as line hotels in Company Baug. Seasonally, they also get shaadi-party work. Local employers and their agents arrive early in the morning around 5 AM, while the outstation employers arrive in the afternoon. The line hotel work includes not only include cooking and other services, but also carrying goods from pickup points to the hotels. He remembers travelling to Gujarat in a truck to work at a dhaba. They were offered Rs. 350–400 for a day's work, in addition to food and accommodation. The accommodation, however, was in a temple beside the dhaba where they worked. Their work included transporting goods from Delhi to Gujarat. Around 15 of them were picked up from Company Baug as *masalchi*, a position that was described to entail only doing the dishes. At the dhaba, however, they had to work for 12 hours without rest in the first shift. The second shift started at eight in the evening and continued till next morning. They did not have much choice about which shift to take up. The wages and timings would vary depending on the hotels, their size and location. As per Ashok's estimates, one would be able to earn Rs. 8,000–9,000 a month from hotel/dhaba work. The wages are either paid on a daily or monthly basis. Sometimes an extra amount is paid to buy alcohol.

Ashok prefers working in shaadi parties because the pay is higher, even though the working hours are much longer. The wage theft is rarer in shaadi-party work compared to the hotel industry. He describes his tasks in these wedding parties as follows:

> We have to do loading and unloading work at night. You get food only when they wish to feed you. That too just *dal chawal* or *khichdi*, mostly. After eating, you get to sleep for a while. When it is around 4 AM, they start screaming "*chalo-chalo*". That is our cue to get inside the truck. People are already half dead because it is so cold in the morning. We keep asking the caterers for blankets; we only get them if they are kind enough. Otherwise, we would be shivering for hours on end, sitting in the back of the truck. Once we reach the venue, we have to unload all the crockery, plates, stands, etc., and set them in their respective spots. Dustbin here, stand there—like that.

Ashok usually goes back home to attend festivals. He could not go back the last Diwali because he had not managed to save enough money. He was looking forward to earning some extra income in the coming wedding season and going home during Holi, his favourite festival.

Raju Khalko[14]

We spoke to Raju Khalko near the Company Baug labour chowk, a place he says he does not like, and that lakhs of people come there to find work. He works in hotels/dhabas or in the shaadi-party line of work but eventually wants to save enough money to go back home.

---

14 Interview taken in March 2019

Raju's home is seven kilometres away from the city of Siliguri in West Bengal, where his mother and father both work as tea-plantation workers. His mother's job is to pick leaves for which she is paid Rs. 5,000 a month. His father works in the plantation company and is paid Rs. 7,000–8,000. Raju also used to work there as a daily-wage worker and used to work the night shift between 11 PM and 7 AM, for which he was paid Rs. 150 rupees per day. He explained that the permanent workers at the plantation would work during the day, while the daily wagers worked at night. The different jobs at the plantation included loading and unloading the picked leaves, as well as packing and processing. Raju's task was to dump the leaves in the machine in order for them to be crushed. When we asked him which community he belongs to, he did not directly answer the question but responded that all the villagers there are Adivasis.

Raju and his family were given quarters inside the plantation by the company, and his family had also built a small house. They also used to work in the agricultural fields during the monsoon, on mostly food crops. One day, in a state of intoxication, Raju had a fight with his mother regarding their finances. After that, he left Siliguri, working in many places (like Gujarat and Punjab) and doing different kinds of work (such as in a factory) before coming to Delhi. In Gujarat, Raju had an accident while operating a machine, and the company paid for his treatment. In Daman and Diu, he worked as an operator for a company in 2012. Raju worked in Punjab for 4-5 years as a tractor driver, for which he earned Rs. 6,000 a month. He used to live near Amritsar in an accommodation provided by his *maalik* (employer) along with a few others. His employer would give them food once a day, and they also used to cook for themselves. When Raju fell sick, he asked for an advance, but his request was denied. He had to spend Rs. 6,000 out of his own pocket for his treatment.

Raju came to Delhi and started working at Janak Cinema with other people from his village. He had to leave after being diagnosed with Tuberculosis. He later began looking for work at the labour chowk. At the Company Baug labour chowk, Raju gets different kinds of jobs, one of which is in the hotel line. Raju had gotten work at a Chhattarpur dhaba, but he ran away from there because of how endless and tiresome the work was. It would start at 7 AM and go on till even 12:30 AM. Raju and his co-workers would get to eat and then lie down only by 1:30 or 2 AM, though they would be able to fall asleep only an hour later. When asked if he ever got to sit during his working hours, he shot back a 'what are you saying?' He estimated that he must have walked around 25 km every day, walking and working in the dhaba. As explained in the beginning of the report, he was a *paani pyaaz wala* and would be paid around Rs. 300 per day. Raju got this job through an agent, who would charge between Rs. 100–200 as commission.

Raju also works in the shaadi-party line from Company Baug. He came to know about the shaadi-party work from residents in a shelter where he was living. He explained that in the wedding season, the workers get paid Rs. 1,000–1,500 and during off-season they are paid Rs. 400–700. The work includes loading and unloading of the utensils, picking up garbage, clearing plates, serving food, replenishing fresh glasses, and also doing the dishes (masalchi). For one party, Raju explained, at least 50 workers are required, and the work is for more than 24 hours, starting one morning and ending the next morning. The work can either be at a farmhouse, where all things needed for the party have to be transported by labourers; or at a banquet hall, where all the things required are already present. The workers are picked up from the labour chowk in a car, but the nature of the work required is not explained to them. The workers are expected to do whatever work is allotted to them. Raju says, 'When we are taken for work, we are not treated like humans. Sometimes our money gets stolen, mobile gets stolen.'

Once Raju was picked by a *seth* along with another worker and was asked to work for one day for which he was promised Rs. 300. Raju did not ask the *seth* any questions about the work. Both the workers were taken to Janakpuri and worked till 12 AM, making *tawa roti* and *parathas* in the night but were eventually only paid Rs. 100 and were told that they would be paid the remainder when the *seth* came next time.

Raju looked for permanent work but did not find any. He told us several times that he wants to save up enough money to be able to go back home. He will have to take a train from New Delhi or Old Delhi Railway Station; a ticket to his hometown costs Rs. 500, but he does not want to head back with only that much. When he used to work in Gujarat, he was able to send money home, but he is unable to save money in Delhi. He borrows Rs. 100–200 from someone at the labour chowk when necessary. His money is spent on his health; sometimes it has been stolen. Once, Raju had worked for 50 hours continuously and went back to the shelter very tired. He had Rs. 5,000 with him, and so did his co-worker. While Raju was asleep, his coworker stole half the money and ran away. Raju went looking for him but could not find him. He had trusted the man because he had bought food for Raju a few times. Raju adds, '… but then I think, maybe he was more desperate than me.' After that incident, Raju felt low for many days; he would go eat in the gurdwara. He later started working at a cement shop for a monthly wage, but he fell sick again. His reports showed that he had anaemia. He was on medication for a month and a half, and soon recovered.

Every day, Raju wakes up at 6 AM and gets ready, taking a bath with cold water even in winter months. He walks two kilometres to Company Baug with three-four people who live with him, hoping to get work by 9 AM and earn Rs. 700–800 for the day. When he does not have any money, he eats at the gurdwara or the Hanuman *mandir*. Raju has no identity documents and has no phone, so his family does not have any phone number to call him on. His main desire is to save enough money to go back home and re-join work at the plantation. He will get his father's job after he retires. His grandfather also did the same job. Raju prefers life in the village where he says they at least have enough food and someone to care for them. He dislikes the labour chowk because there is a lot of infighting and alcoholism here. Raju himself only drinks once in 3-4 months and does not want to become addicted to alcohol. He does not think that the labour chowk should be there. But for now, that is where he works.

3.8.   On Aspirations and Moving to the City

Rahul Kumar[15]

Rahul Kumar came to the city of Delhi six years ago after fighting with his *chachaji* (uncle). In his desire to prove that he can do and 'become' something, he left his village with just Rs. 10–20 in his pocket. Rahul's village is near Bina in the Sagar district of Madhya Pradesh. Back in his village, his family owns land that measures less than an acre (roughly 3-4 bighas). Rahul does not look after the land; his grandfather usually handles all the farming work. Rahul's family consists of his parents, his brothers and sisters, and his uncle. The traditional occupation of his family is farming but since they are solely dependent on the rains for irrigation, it is a difficult process throughout the year. Rahul's family cannot afford a borewell, so they don't own one. The crops are usually destroyed without water. They grow wheat only in the monsoon because it requires a lot of water; in other months they grow *makai* (corn) and *sarso* (mustard), which do not need as much water. Rahul explains that it is not easy to earn money from agriculture, which is why people from the village migrate to Mumbai, Bangalore, or Delhi to earn a living. He emphasizes that in their village, if one has land and does agriculture, then they can sustain themselves, otherwise they migrate to the city as a rule. In the city, he says, things like food and even phone services are easily available. In contrast, back in their village, he and his family have to walk three to four kilometres merely to sell their crops.

In the event that their crops fail, the *zamindar* (feudal lord) and the landowners lend them money, with interest. Rahul, however, does not have anything to do with the *len-den* (borrowing and lending money). He says that it is the elders in his family,

---

15 Interview taken in April 2019

mostly his *bade papa* (father's brother), who borrow money and he only knows that moneylenders in the village charge interest. Rahul used to find agricultural work tedious and uninteresting. His uncle wanted him to take care of the land, but Rahul refused and left home. He recalled his first day in Delhi; when he arrived, he did not know anything about the city and the ways in which people live here. Rahul had taken a train to Delhi and upon reaching, he ate something with whatever money he had. He could not figure out what to do after that and spent the night at the railway platform. The next day, he observed that people around him were engaged in drinking alcohol and smoking all the time. He did not know anything about the different kinds of *nasha* (addictions), he said. Rahul was scared and remained hungry the entire day.

For several days, Rahul slept on the platform; one day, a man came and slept next to him. They began talking and Rahul shared his problems with him, telling him that he had come from a village, had no money and no food. That man took him to a gurudwara where they ate together. Rahul expressed his desire to work, and his companion offered to help him. He directed Rahul to simply stay with him, and so Rahul did, on the footpaths of Chandni Chowk, for the next 15–20 days. The man paid for Rahul's food and also rented blankets and mattresses from Chandni Chowk for both of them to share. Then one day, he offered to take Rahul along to work with him, directing him to simply observe what he does. It was that day that Rahul realized that his companion was a petty thief and engaged in, what Rahul called, *galat kaam* (wrongdoing). He was scared, but that night, the man offered Rahul a drink and both of them went to sleep. Rahul confronted him the next morning, telling him that he was scared and had never done such things before. When the man made their togetherness contingent upon Rahul's engagement in this 'work', Rahul left him.

Rahul then came to Yamuna Pushta, near Kashmere Gate. He recalled there being no shelter homes or *rain basera* (night shelters) there at the time with one exception, *'parde wala ka'*. He remembers that a lot of the region was forested. After staying there for 3-4 days, someone suggested that he could find work in shaadi parties if he went to Company Baug. Rahul went to the Company Baug labour chowk, but no one came to hire for that line of work that day. Instead, Rahul got work as a *mistri* (mason) doing *beldaari ka kaam* (shoveling work). The wage was Rs. 110 that day, said Rahul, remarking that the same work now fetches a wage of Rs. 450 per day.

Although Rahul was taken for *beldaari ka kaam,* he did not know anything about that particular skill. He was told to mix the masala but was unable to do it properly. His employers realized that he was new to the work and supported him in picking up the skill. He was given Rs. 60 daily for his basic needs and was told that he could collect the rest of the money (Rs. 50) if he came the next day. Each day, Rahul needed the money, so he went to work again, and his employer gave him the remaining money each day. He worked between 10 AM and 5 PM every day for four days, and then went back home.

After returning home, Rahul felt that if he stayed back in his village, he wouldn't earn any money. He felt uneasy and began crying. After that, he started commuting to Delhi from his village, covering a distance of 240 km, which took him seven hours by train. He got work from the labour chowk two-three more times. Sometimes he would assist the head mason or do the brick laying as well as plastering work. Rahul also worked wedding parties. He worked at a hotel in Bahadurgarh, Haryana for four months and was hired from Company Baug for Rs. 250 per day. But when asked whether he received his full payment, Rahul said, 'they kept my Rs. 3,000.'

Rahul's first hotel job was at a line hotel. He had gone to this hotel with two other hires from Company Baug. The two other persons with Rahul later ran away but Rahul stayed as he needed money. He was made to work as the *paani pyaaz wala,* where his task was to clean the table and bring a plate of onions and water for new customers. After four days, his *maalik* liked his work and employed him as a waiter (which Rahul described as *service ka kaam)* for 10 days. After 10 days, his employer observed that Rahul is hardworking, and Rahul's stipulated task was changed again. He was put on night duty, where he made tea for the workers, cut vegetables, and served food if any customers came at night. There were four people working at the *dhaba*: two service waiters, a *masalchi,* and Rahul.

Rahul's employer had then asked him to collect and keep an account of all the money earned at night and to submit it to him the next morning. When Rahul was asked whether his *maalik* was good, Rahul replied, 'Yes, but he kept Rs. 3,000 of mine with him, saying "you have to come back here for work when you come back from home," but Rahul did not feel like going back to that line of work.

He explained that from the Company Baug labour chowk, most people get work in the shaadi-party line of work, where the average daily wage is Rs. 400–500. There is a distinction between shaadi-party work at a banquet hall and at farmhouses. In the latter, a large part of their work is loading and unloading as farmhouses do not contain furniture, utensils, and other required items. As per Rahul, the daily rate for work at a farmhouse is Rs. 700–800 and the loading-unloading work is carried out by JDC, Bharat or RK. Since there is no loading-unloading work required at banquet halls, the daily rate is lower. At farmhouses, the workers do the loading and unloading during the day and at night, they carry out 'local service' that involved serving food and also cleaning up at the same time. Rahul emphasized that there is more work at the farmhouse and therefore the pay is Rs. 700–800.

Generally, the shaadi-party line of work consists of two shifts, one during the day when things are set up, and the other at night when the workers perform the local work. There is another classification of work in this line which delineates the kind of work performed. One is the 'local caterer'and the other is the 'service caterer.' The service caterers, as Rahul explained, serve food and drinks while the local caterer sets the tables, picks up glasses, cleans the tables and the dishes. Rahul told us that Delhi is famous for shaadi-party work, and there might be around 100 or 150 thekedars, which is why people come here to hire labour for shaadi-party work.

Rahul emphasizes that regular work is very difficult to find. He lives alone at the night shelter, which is about two to three kilometres away from the labour chowk. He does not have any relatives in the city and goes back home twice or thrice a year. The most common and efficient way to find work, Rahul explains, is through the labour chowk. One may reach out to a contractor and even develop good relations with one, but mostly, contractors hire workers from the labour chowk. Though the average wage set by the government is Rs. 540 per day, workers are only paid Rs. 300–350 since the intermediaries take some of it as commission. At Company Baug, the *dalaals* (brokers) charge the employers/contractors a commission of Rs. 100 per person. Rahul insists that workers do not take advance from employers because it takes the form of a debt trap. 'I have seen it. You will have to keep working for them,' says Rahul.

Rahul's brother-in-law has a government job in Nainital that pays Rs. 8,000 a month, and also gets other facilities from the government such as accommodation, water, and electricity. For Rahul, that is an ideal mode of employment. Rahul also worked a regular job in Mumbai once, where he had accompanied an acquaintance from his village. There, he worked as a lift operator and earned Rs. 12,500 a month. He recounts that in Mumbai, he would make Rs. 500 from the labour chowk, but also that Mumbai is a very expensive city.

When asked if he thinks that the workers in Delhi are paid a fair wage, Rahul said, 'No. If you give us Rs. 500 and ask us to work all day and all night long, of course that is really less. But it is a *majboori* (compulsion)'. He went on to talk about the lack of unity among workers and said, 'If I ask for fairer wages, they will all keep quiet. Once the work is over, they might even beat me up. And they will not pay.'

Rahul says that sometimes his employers might withhold a certain portion of his final payment and promise to pay it when he returns to them for work, but it has never happened that he was not paid for his work. He says he has heard several stories about workers not being paid, being tied up and kept hostage, especially in Haryana. He says that 60% of the employers pay while about 40% of the persons do not pay and are, what he calls, scoundrels.

Talking about unpaid work, Rahul brought up the question of, in his words, 'drama'. He explained that many workers drink alcohol and then 'do drama', saying that they were not paid by their employers. He opines that both sides, the workers as well as their employers, are at fault. He faults the workers for keeping the money in their pockets instead of putting it away safely, thereby inviting pickpockets and frauds to take advantage of them. Although he drinks too, Rahul insists that he does not 'do drama'. He wakes up at 6 AM and walks to the labour chowk; 8 or 9 AM is too late to find work. Rahul drinks tea in the morning only if he has Rs. 5–10 to spare. He waits at the labour chowk till 10 or 10:30 AM, after which no one comes to hire workers. Anyone who comes later usually pays less. If an employer is hiring in an emergency, he might pay up to Rs. 1,000, while the usual rate is Rs. 500–700. If Rahul ever has an accident at work, which usually involves a normal cut, burn or fever, his *maalik* pays for the treatment. Last year, he contracted tuberculosis and is still taking medication for it. Whenever workers get hired, they are given food three times a day as well as a place to sleep. Rahul lives in the shelter but says that one could sleep anywhere. He finds the shelter disturbing and tiresome as there are many people around who talk and share their stories. He also does not find any work near the shelter. In the six years that Rahul has been here, he has never sent any money to his family, except for a few money orders that he sends during weddings. He has never taken a loan.

When asked whether the labour chowk should exist, Rahul said that he does not have a specific problem with the labour chowk. He recounted his first day in Delhi six years ago, after he ran away from his family. He had no work, no food and someone had suggested to him to go find work at Company Baug. Rahul said, '*Aisi jagah honi chahiye ke aate hi bande ko kaam mil jaye*' (there should be such places where a person can go and find work immediately).

When asked if he prefers the village or the city, Rahul said that he surely likes the village more.

3.9.   On Wage Theft

Ankit Gaud[16]

> Interviewer: What kind of work do you do?
>
> Ankit: Whatever work I get. *Party ka kaam, hotel line ka kaam.* If I don't get work, then I don't.
>
> Interviewer: What do you do on days you do not get any work?
>
> Ankit: I sleep on the footpath or in a *rain basera.*

When Ankit first came to Delhi, the first place he went to was a Gurdwara. He had no money. He had walked 22 km on foot to reach Sabarmati station in Gujarat, then travelled to the capital in a parcel van. He reached Delhi at 10 PM, starving, having had nothing to eat in two days.

> Do you know if someone starves for two days, they won't be able to eat when they get food? I managed to eat two rotis in that Gurudwara with great difficulty. When we arrived, we didn't know where to go. There were three of us—I am from UP, one is from Mumbai, and one from Delhi. The guy from Delhi, he used to be homeless. You know what homeless means, right? He was a beggar, but he knew where to get free food. So we went to a Gurdwara that first night.

Ankit came to Delhi from Siddharth Nagar, Gujarat. Back in his village, he lived with his mother and his four brothers. They own two to three bighas of land where they grow wheat, mustard, *mattar* (peas), and have their own pond. When his father died, he borrowed money from his relatives. However, Ankit and his brothers had to drop out of school, and his elder brother started doing carpentry in Mumbai.

When he started working, Ankit was offered Rs. 2,000–3,000 a month by a *chaiwala* (tea seller). He asked, 'What will I do with

---

16 Interview taken in March 2019

Rs. 3,000 a month?' and was thrown out. Since then, he has been looking for work. He was found by a thekedar who hired him for wedding party work. Initially, his job was to pick up dirty dishes and clean them. He was disgusted by this work, but desperate for money, so he continued to do it. After 5–10 days, when he left the job, he was only paid Rs. 100 for all the work. Ankit used the money to get a haircut. He came to know that the thekedar had held back the payment of everyone who was working there and owed Rs. 17,000–18,000 to some people. When others came to him and told him that they were not being paid their share, he said, 'Brothers, what are you doing? Come with me.' That is when they decided to leave for Delhi.

In Delhi, after going to the Gurudwara, they went to the Pushta, where they slept that night. The next morning, they went looking for work but returned unsuccessful. So they went to Gandhi Nagar, where they found work for pushing carts loaded with goods. Ankit refused to do it as it was impossible for him in the hot weather. He would faint. One of his group members took up the job and pushed the cart from Gandhi Nagar in East Delhi to Mittayi, for which he was paid Rs. 120. He bought Ankit food from this money, which Ankit later felt guilty for 'shamelessly eating'. After that, Ankit started to pull the cart as well. It was backbreaking work for a meagre Rs. 25 per hour.

After working, they would buy some *ganja* (cannabis). Ankit had started smoking with them too. From the Rs. 25 he had earned, he bought a bottle of water for Rs. 10 and poured it on his head. This helped him cool down a bit. He bought two beedi bundles and one matchbox with the rest of the money and was left with four rupees. He sat there, in a park, smoking away. He was finding it fun, the way the smoke was circling in the air. 'So one after another, I finished the entire bundle...' His friends asked him, 'Where did you get the money to smoke?' Ankit told them about the Rs. 25. They gave him six more rupees and asked him to fetch tea. Then they all had a meal at the Hanuman Mandir and went to sleep.

Over the last five years in Delhi, Ankit has worked at labour chowks, done shaadi-party work. He has stayed at gurdwaras and temples. He has moved from one place to another, eating and drinking, working wherever he has been able to find the means to survive or secure a job. He and his friends who came from Sabarmati are more often than not underpaid for their labour and face wage theft at the hands of thekedars and employers. He wants to go home but feels ashamed for not having sent any money all these years. There is no factory in his village so he would either have to do construction work, shopkeeping, or agricultural work with his family. In the village, only the Tiwaris and a couple of other upper caste communities are land-owning and have enough to sustain themselves.

3.10. On Uncertainties of Work and Life

Pappu[17]

> Interviewer: Where are you living in Delhi?

> Pappu: I am in Bawana these days. If I get work, then let's see where I'll move.

Mohammad Kamre Alam, or Pappu, as he calls himself, is a resident of JJ Colony, Bawana. He is from Kolkata, West Bengal, and owns land in Bihar ('2-3 bighas maximum,' he told us), but Pappu has lived in Delhi for about 18 years. He first lived in Shantivan Jhuggi but when that colony was demolished, he shifted to Bawana. Pappu's time in Delhi has been riddled with uncertainties—being forced to move out of Shantivan to Bawana because of demolition, and moving between Kolkata, Delhi, and even once to Chennai to get work. Like him, many people migrate from certain regions of Bihar and UP looking for work.

His sister also lives in Bawana, while his aunt, uncle, and grandmother are back in Kolkata. His brother lives in their house in Bihar and they have leased their land to someone else for agri-

---

17   Interview taken in February 2019

culture work. Because of floods and water accumulation on farmland, they can only grow rice.

Pappu has been involved in different kinds of work after leaving his village—when he first came to Bawana, he lived with his sister and worked with her in handicrafts, making earrings and nose rings for women. Then he worked to make bags and money purses. This was in Kapashera, where he was paid Rs. 2,200–2,300. He then started doing loading work involving tables, chairs, and newspaper bundles.

Pappu shared that ever since he started doing loading work, his health has not been good. His wife died four years ago after contracting an infection during childbirth. She stopped eating over the years and fell sick, eventually succumbing to her ill health. His son lives with his mother-in-law. Ever since his wife died, Pappu's health has also declined. He is no longer able to send money home like he used to. He is HIV positive and possibly has tuberculosis; much of his savings go into medical expenses. Even when his wife was ill, he spent most of his earnings on her medical treatment.

Pappu also does shaadi-party work. He told us that it is 'more work and less pay.' He knows that if he does the same work in some hotel, he would be better paid and would even get lunch. But in party work he has to be careful and make sure he eats in a corner, ensuring that nobody sees him. The workers fear that if someone sees them eating, they might get beaten up. Though they get the money on time, what they get paid is not enough.

3.11.   On Friendships and Relationships that Help us Survive

Jagdeesh[18]

'People make friends very quickly here…we have to make new relations here to sustain ourselves.'

---

18   Interview taken in February 2019

Jagdeesh has built his life in Delhi based on relations of trust. Apart from his brother who lives here, there are several people whom he is friends with. He says that he needs this for survival. He has friends from his time at Yamuna Pushta with whom he roams around often, and they occasionally lend him Rs. 100–200. There is also 'Mummy' at the tea shop, with whom some of the workers leave their money for safekeeping. Jagdeesh says that when he needs some money, he can rely on them. 'We have to trust people here. If they take advantage of me, there is nothing I can do.'

Jagdeesh came to Delhi seven years ago. His brother repairs computers and mobile phones in Azadpur. Jagdeesh was not encouraged to study when he was young, because his father wanted him to work on the farm. He does not know how to read and write, and does not have a bank account, so he borrows money from his brother or his friends.

When he was back in his village, some people made Jagdeesh fill a few forms through which he was hired to build mobile towers in Delhi. But when he arrived, he found that there was no work for him. That is when, out of necessity, he had to go to the labour chowk. He has had many different jobs in Delhi—washing dishes, riding a cycle rickshaw, working on a farm in Haryana, construction work, and shaadi-party work. For a month he washed dishes at a dhaba and earned Rs. 350–400 rupees a day. Jagdeesh says he liked this job the most because he was allowed to rest between loads. But usually, his work hours are around 16 hours a day, till 12:00 AM.

It is difficult to know whom to trust in the labour chowks, especially for a newcomer. Though there is work available in the Company Baug labour chowk, Jagdeesh says he now prefers going to a contractor he trusts. Through a contractor, he can get work for a longer, continuous period like 15 or 20 days, along with food and accommodation. But contractors also charge the worker a commission. If the normal rate of is Rs. 1,000, the contractor would keep Rs. 100 rupees and give Jagdeesh Rs. 900. This is the cost Jagdeesh pays for getting regular work. According to him, if the contractor does not take this responsibility of giving work, he might end up sitting idle.

Another relationship that has enabled Jagdeesh to survive the harsh city life is with his brother. In the beginning, when he arrived in Delhi, he lived with his brother and sister-in-law and their children. They paid Rs. 2,500 in rent for the room. Jagdeesh initially struggled to find work. When his brother suggested that he go to the Company Baug labour chowk, he went and found some work at a farm in Haryana, where he was paid Rs. 30,000 for four months. It was backbreaking work that started at four in the morning and went on till seven in the evening. He worked in the field cutting grass all day. The money that he earned from that job, he sent to his brother to send home. Though his family owns about six to seven acres of land, they earn no profit from the land. They get back as much as they spend and sometimes the cost is more than the earnings. Sometimes there is flood, sometimes drought. This is why he sends money back home from Delhi.

Jagdeesh now lives in a shelter near the Company Baug chowk. When he first came to Delhi, he was living on the railway platform. Someone told him about the shelter, and he stayed there for a few days. He washed dishes there for three-four days and earned some money, so he was able to reach his brother. He says this shelter is better than the others, which don't let people in after 7 PM. Since coming to Delhi, his life has involved moving from one job to another, one place to another, much like the rest of the workers in the chowk. But he says he is getting tired of the place. He wants to go home.

Mohan[19]

'Why do people come to the labour chowk?'

'People come here, firstly, because they need the money. Secondly, some people do drugs. They need money for alcohol and

---

19   Interview taken in February 2019

ganja. And thirdly, there are people who don't do any drugs but save money and spend on food.'

This is what Mohan told us when we began our conversation with him about his life in Delhi and the Company Baug labour chowk. Mohan has been in Delhi for 20 years and has been observing the labour chowk since the year 2000. He has observed many things about how the transactions here work—how the workers come from every neighbouring state (Punjab, Haryana, UP), what kind of work is the best or fetches the most money, and how the contractors try to extract more and more money from the transactions, treating them as though they are trading the human beings themselves, and not just their labour.

Mohan left his village and came to Delhi in the year 2000. He doesn't remember his village. He never saw his mother, although he remembers his father. His father was a rickshaw driver, who earned anywhere from Rs. 80–150 in a day, depending on the *sawaari* (customers) he would get. Mohan's siblings live back in their village Kunjpura in Haryana. One of his sisters is married and stays in her marital home in Uttar Pradesh. They are Dalits, and do not own any land in the village. They earn money by working as labourers, making *Gud* (jaggery) from sugarcane and sugarcane farming. He told us that when there is too much rain during the wheat harvest, it can damage crops and lead to a loss of livelihood. But the government does nothing to help the landowners or agricultural workers during those times.

In 2000, Mohan came to Delhi with a friend, looking for work opportunities. His friend used to work in wedding parties. Mohan also mentioned another person who used to do some 'illegal work' in Old Delhi. He would feed Mohan and take him to the park with him and ask him to wait. Mohan worked in the hotels and slept there.

In the beginning, he stayed in Old Delhi on the *patri* (footpath). Mohan told us that sometimes there were *lalas* (businessmen) who would distribute food, and other times they would eat in the Sis Ganj Gurdwara. But they faced a lot of problems sleeping on the footpath. It would get too cold in the winters and rain heavily in the monsoons, so they would buy sacks and use them for cover. No one helped them at that time.

Mohan has been going to Company Baug for the past seven years. He used to do heavy labour like *dhakka* (public carrier) work from Azad Market to Tokri Mohalla for Rs. 10 per *thela* (cart). This would earn him about Rs. 70–80 rupees per day. He also went for shaadi-party work, where the daily wage was Rs. 200. He has also worked in chai shops and hotels. Hotel work fetches about Rs. 300–400 a day, while tea shops pay workers Rs. 600 per month. When he has no work at all, he eats and sleeps in the Gurudwara nearby.

Mohan typically wakes up at six in the morning to leave early for Company Baug. He stays there till ten, by which time a contractor could come to hire workers. He reaches early, though those seeking work keep pouring in till 9 AM. There are always about 40-50 people at Company Baug looking for work. He described to us how some contractors looking to hire labourers engaged in wage theft:

> Sometimes, there are agents who would do the wrong thing and practically sell off the labourer. The employer would take him and make him work. If the worker asked for money, then the employer would say he has already paid the agent for a full year of work.

Mohan told us that he prefers the work of washing dishes for fruit or tikki-chaat stalls. In the hotel line of work, he wakes up at seven in the morning, cleans the dishes used at night and prepares breakfast by ten. He has also done the work of making rotis in a tandoor, serving tables, frying *dal* and *sabji*. The work is from 7 AM to 11 PM or even midnight. Shaadi-party work has similar timings—he leaves at 8 AM and works till 11 PM or midnight.

During the course of our conversation, Mohan told us he had not been in good health. He had just recovered from TB but is also HIV positive. He cannot do heavy lifting work. He also had an accident at Company Baug some years ago where he was hit by a car. He never found the man who hit him because he fled before Mohan could note the car's registration number. Though he recovered in a month, it was difficult for him. He used to be able to save money but his capacity to work has significantly reduced in the recent years, so he is unable to save any money now. He has not seen or called his sister also and has not visited her in UP in 15 years because he is unable to save much money.

The way Mohan described his own and others' life in the labour chowk is very functional: people come to the labour chowk because they need money. He has little memory of his life before the labour chowk, before the daily grind in Old Delhi. Despite having sustained an injury and contracted contagious diseases during his time here, he has no choice but to stay and continue working day after day, for his own survival.

4

Findings From the Survey[20]

In an attempt to understand the conditions of the workers, a survey was conducted in Sarai Kale Khan labour chowk and Company Baug labour chowk. We took a sample of 430 workers, of which 224 were from Company Baug and 206 from Sarai Kale Khan. The samples were collected over 10 days to understand their working hours, role of middlemen, gendered vulnerabilities, caste and religious composition, housing options, migration patterns, etc. As the population in labour chowks is transitory in nature, the sampling was random. The data might not represent the condition of workers in all labour chowks across Delhi since the work is seasonal. It should be noted that most of the respondents were migrants. Out of all the respondents from the two labour chowks, only 7 out of 430 were born in Delhi.

Out of the 376 samples taken, 42.33% were General Category, 24.19% were OBC, 19.30% were SC, 2.33% were ST and 11.86% of the workers preferred not to disclose their caste. The religious composition of the sampled workers was predominantly Hindu (86.51%). 10.93% were Muslim, 0.47% were Christian, 0.2% were Buddhist, 0.2 % were Sikh, 0.2% were Sindhi, 0.2% were Jain and 1.16% preferred not to answer. Only 42 of them were women, of

---

20 Acknowledging the assistance of Mr. Ruzel Shreshta in analysing the data

whom 41 were from the Sarai Kale Khan labour chowk. Company Baug labour chowk had only one woman respondent.

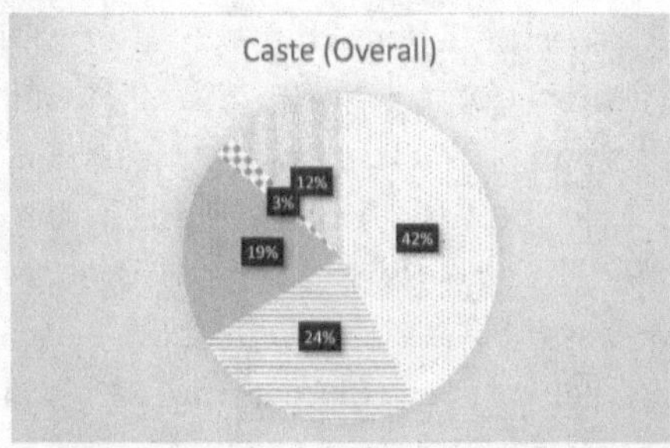

	Overall
General Category	42.33
OBC	24.19
SC	19.3
ST	2.33
Do not prefer to answer	11.86

Occupational categories in the labour chowks

The workers in Sarai Kale Khan were mostly primarily engaged in construction work, whereas at Company Baug labour chowk the respondents either worked in shaadi-party work or catering / dhaba work.

In Sarai Kale Khan, 86.66 % said construction was their primary occupation, and 0.57% said it was their tertiary occupation. 7.39% said shaadi-party work was their primary occupation, 12.5% said it was their secondary occupation, and 2.27% said it was their tertiary occupation. Furthermore, 6.25% said dhaba work was their primary occupation, 5.68% said it was their secondary occupation, 1.14% said it was their tertiary occupation. Lastly, 1.14% said loading and unloading was their primary occupation, 10.8% said it was their secondary occupation, 2.27% said it was their tertiary occupation and 0.57% said it was their fourth preference.

Occupation for Sarai Kale Khan*

	1	2	3	4
Construction	84.66%	0.57%		
Shaadi-party	7.39%	12.50%	2.27%	
Dhaba	6.25%	5.68%	1.14%	
Loading-unloading	1.14%	10.80%	2.27%	0.57%

In Company Baug, 11.11% of the workers said construction was their primary occupation, 5.82% said it was their secondary occupation, 1.06% said it was their tertiary occupation and 1.06% said it was their fourth preference of occupation. In this labour chowk, 63.49% said shaadi-party work was their primary occupation, 13.23% said that it was their secondary occupation and 0.53% said it was their tertiary occupation. At the same labour chowk, 19.05% said working in dhabas was their primary occupation, 18.52 % said it was their secondary occupation, 0.53% said that it was their tertiary occupation. 6.35% said loading and unloading was their primary occupation, 4.23% said it was their secondary occupation, and 6.35% said it was their tertiary occupation.

Occupation For Company Baug*

	1	2	3	4
Construction	11.11%	5.82%	1.06%	1.06%
Shaadi-party	63.49%	13.23%	0.53%	
Dhaba	19.05%	18.52%	0.53%	
Loading-unloading	6.35%	4.23%	6.35%	

Seasonality of employment

A considerable number of workers at the Sarai Kale Khan labour chowk were farmers or agricultural workers who returned home during the agricultural season. These numbers were slightly lower at the Company Baug labour chowk. In Company Baug, 30% said they return home during the agricultural season and 70% said they don't go home for the agricultural season. At the Sarai Kale Khan labour chowk, 41% said they go home for agriculture and 59% said they don't go home even during the agricultural season. This pattern confirms the link between the agrarian crisis and the urban informal sector.

Further, around 69% of the respondents said that earning extra income was one of the reasons for working at the labour chowk. Around 50% of the respondents said that unavailability of

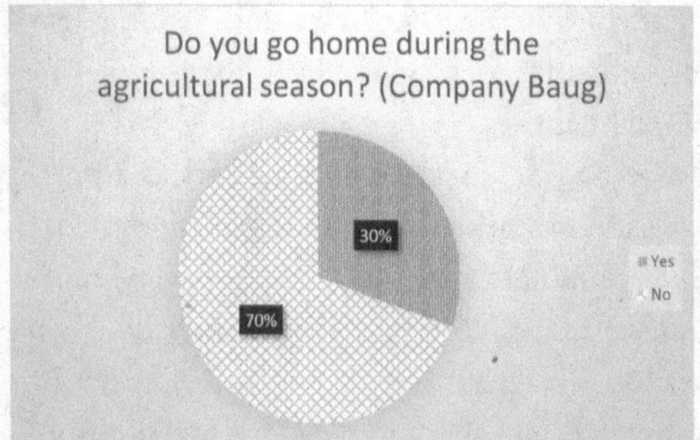

Company Baug	
Yes	67
No	153

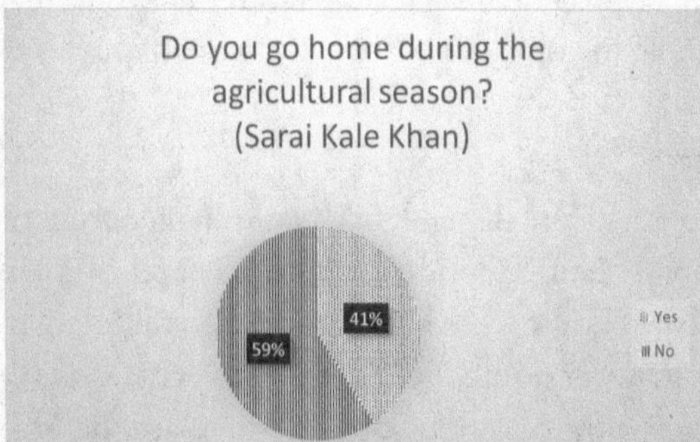

Sarai Kale Khan	
Yes	84
No	122

work was one of the reasons (out of several reasons) for migrating and working at the labour chowk. 29% of the respondents said that insufficient income from agriculture was one of the reasons for migrating. Around 1.7% of the respondents said that the reason for migration was because of loss of livelihood in their home.

According to our survey, the workers manage to save very little money. From the sampled workers, around 41% said they had no savings. Among the rest, the savings varied from a few hundred rupees a month to Rs. 7,000–8,000 a month. There were a few outliers who managed to save over Rs. 10,000 a month.

Whatever little savings the workers could manage, a lot of them sent home. Around 30% of the workers send their money home. Since a few of the migrants actually live with their family, the savings were spent on their family (6.7% said they spent the savings on their family). Around 2.8% of the respondents have said that they put the savings in their bank account. Around 0.93% of the workers (4 respondents) are saving up in hopes of starting their own shop or small business.

An important part of our survey while understanding the conditions of work, was to examine the chances of economic mobility for the workers in pursuit of a steadier income and better living conditions. It is clear that since 41% of the workers don't have savings and those who do send the money home, there is very little room for accumulation. The fact that merely 4 out of 430 respondents are thinking of starting their own shop clearly indicates that the workers are not able to come out of their situation of poverty.

Recruitment practices

A majority of the workers were dependent on middlemen for employment. The Company Baug labour chowk has a couple of main brokers who control the chowk. The thekedars are also middlemen who recruit workers in fewer numbers. There are different kinds of middlemen associated with the labour chowk. There are the brokers who control the labour chowk; petty contractors, or thekedars, who are workers themselves but also recruit other workers to join their team; there are Rajmistris, or skilled workers, who also approach workers; there are also Jamadars, who recruit workers from the source itself. The classification given below is based on how the workers themselves categorised the mode of recruitment.

On the question of where they get work from, 212 workers said that they have gotten work through the thekedar; 165 of the workers said they have gotten work through a broker, 46 workers said that they have gotten work through contacts, 44 workers have gotten work through drive-through (drivers or helpers coming to pick up workers in private vehicles). Three workers said they have gotten work through self-searching, three said they have gotten work by the company, two workers have gotten work directly through the owner and two said they got work through the previous employer.

In Company Baug, 111 workers responded that they have gotten work through the broker, 97 workers have said that they have gotten work through the thekedar, 17 workers have gotten work through contacts, 15 workers through drive-throughs, 2 workers said they got work through the owner, 2 workers got work through previous employers and 1 found work through self-searching.

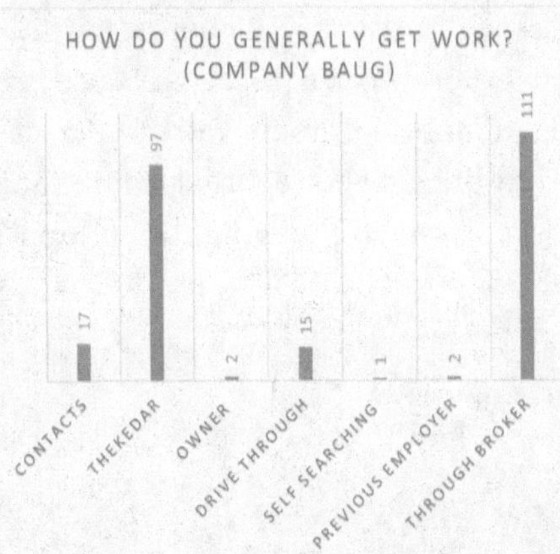

In CBB	
Contacts	17
Thekedar	97
Owner	2
Drive Through	15
Self Searching	1
Previous Employer	2
Through Broker	111
	245

In Sarai Kale Khan, 115 workers said they have gotten work through the thekedar, 54 workers said they have gotten work through the broker, 29 workers said they have gotten work through contacts, 29 workers said they have gotten work through drive-through, 3 workers said they have gotten work being hired by companies and 2 said they have gotten work through self-searching.

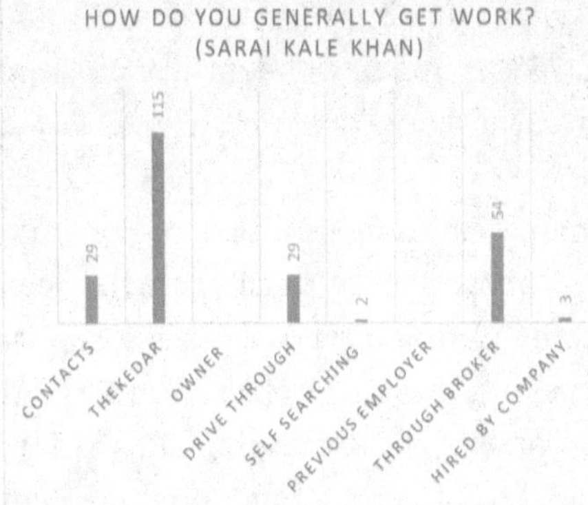

In SKK	
Contacts	29
Thekedar	115
Owner	
Drive Through	29
Self Searching	2
Previous Employer	
Through Broker	54
Hired by Company	3
	232

Overwork, low wages, and wage theft

It was not possible to calculate the average income per person per day since working hours vary across sectors. Overall, the average working hours for workers who reported their primary work to be construction work are 10.73 hours per day. However, in the case of workers who reported shaadi-party as their primary work, the average number of hours worked in a day is 18.09 hours. Furthermore, for respondents who said working at a dhaba was their primary occupation, the average number of hours worked per day was 15.36 hours. In the case of workers who reported loading and unloading as their primary work, the average number of hours worked per day is 11.86 hours.

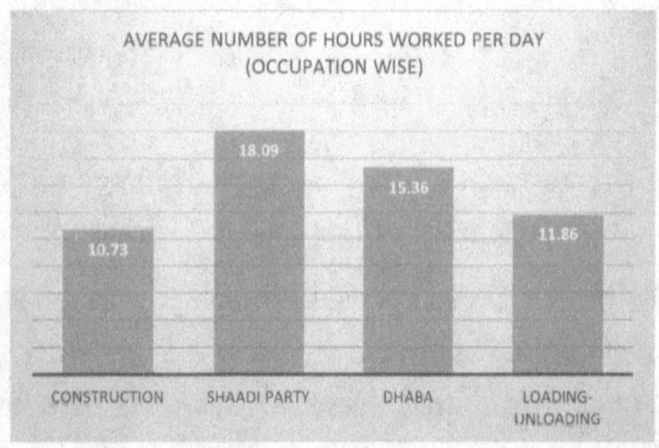

Construction	Shaadi Party	Dhaba	Loading-Unloading
10.73	18.09	15.36	11.86

Not only are the workers overworked, but most of them also do not get paid for extra work. 78% of the respondent workers said that they don't get paid for extra work, while merely 22% said they do.

It is also important to note that there are issues of non-payment. In our survey, 53.3 % of the workers said that there has been at least one instance when they were not paid for the work that they had done. This illustrates the precarity of the workers. At the Sarai Kale Khan labour chowk, 51% of respondent workers reported at least one instance of not getting paid after work. In

Company Baug, the percentage of people not getting paid at least once was 42%.

Among the people who said that there were instances where they were not paid, 71.59% said that there was some form of wage theft, either from the thekedar or the worker. Around 9.7% of them said that they did not get paid since they ran away because of workplace harassment. Around 19% of them said the lack of payment had to do with some kind of misbehaviour from the employer.

Lack of maternal care and childcare

There were a total of 42 women in our sample from the labour chowks. Of these respondents, 41 women were from the Sarai Kale Khan labour chowk, and one was from the Company Baug labour chowk. A large number of women respondents, i.e., 35.71% (15 out of 42) said that they worked during pregnancy.

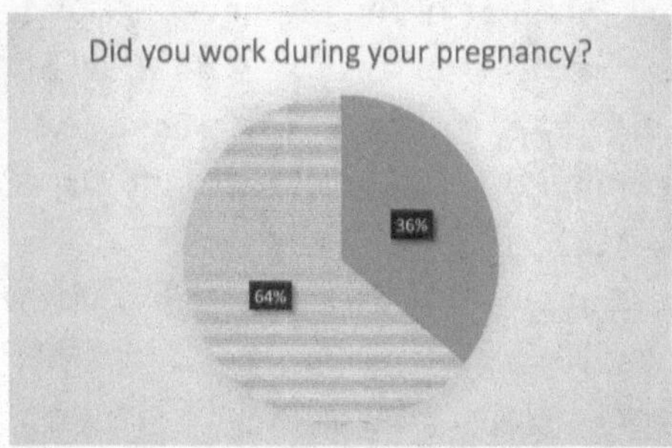

| Yes | 15 |
| No | 27 |

Furthermore, a large number of women reported having worked during pregnancy, with 11 out of 16 respondents having worked during the ninth month of pregnancy. One woman reported having worked till the third month, one until the fourth month, and two women worked up to the fifth month of pregnancy.

Of all the 42 women respondents, 44% women leave their children at the labour camp or in the jhuggi at the workplace, 20% said they leave them with other children, 13% leave their children at the village, 9% said they take turns with their women co-workers to take care of the children, 9% said they leave them with their siblings and 5% of the respondent women leave their kids at the anganwadi.

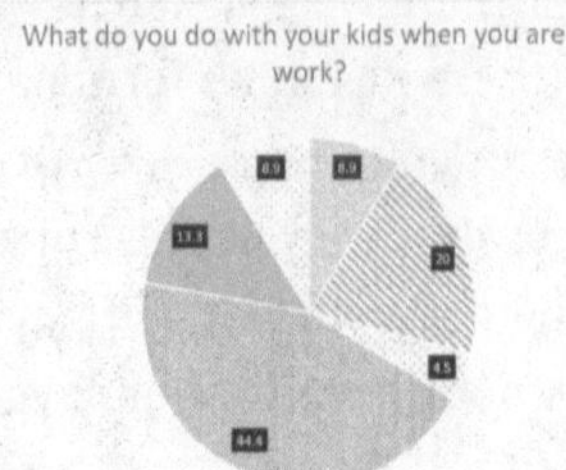

Leave them with siblings	8.9
Leave them at Anganwadi	4.5
Leave them at the Village	13.3
Leave them with other kids	20
Leave them at the labor camp or juggi at the workplace	44.4
Leave them with co-worker on rotation	8.9

Homelessness

Most of the workers at the labour chowks were homeless. When they don't find work, 40.4 % of them live on the streets. However, 39.2% of them live in the shelter homes, and merely 8.2% of the respondents live on rent. Furthermore, only 3.1% of the respondents had their own houses. The rest of the respondents stay in temporary places, such as the bus stop, railway station, labour colony, inside the park, the *godam* (godown), with friends, or at the gurudwara. Some of them also rent a bed for around Rs. 40 a night.

When the workers do find work, 61.2% of them live at the worksite itself. From the rest, 17% of the workers live in the shelter home, 7.2% of them live in a jhuggi provided by the employer, 5.8% of them live on rent, 4.4% of them live on the streets, and merely 1.6% of them live in their own homes. The rest of them, even when they are working, manage in temporary locations which include railway stations, labour camps, *godam* or at the homes of relatives.

Because of the precarious nature of the living conditions of most labour-chowk workers, even basic amenities are not guaranteed. For instance, the safety of personal belongings emerged as a major cause of concern during the survey. Of all the respondents, 67.6% of the respondents reported that they do not have a safe place to keep their money and other important documents.

85.7% of the workers did not have proof of address. Because of this, opening a bank account is difficult. Many workers reported not having bank accounts (63.9%), further exacerbating the issue of lack of safety for their savings. Of these, around 13% of the respondents who do not have an account said that they could not open one because of the lack of such documents, while 17.5% said that they did not have enough savings to open an account.

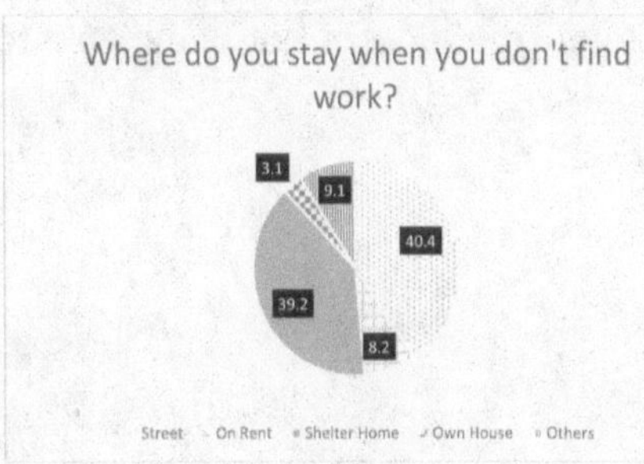

Street	40.4
On Rent	8.2
Shelter Home	39.2
Own House	3.1
Others	9.1

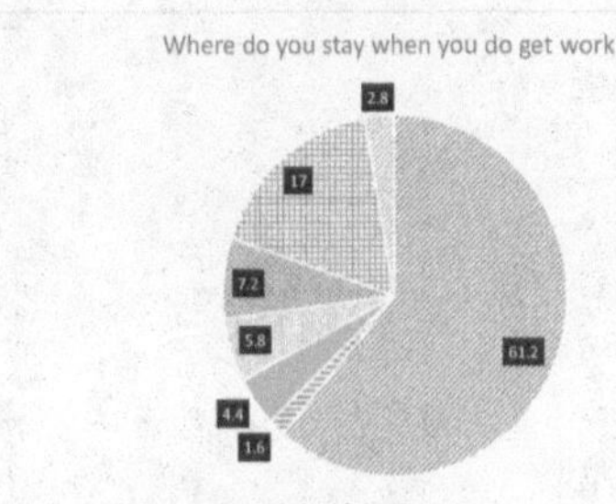

At the workplace	61.2
Own House	1.6
Street	4.4
On rent	5.8
Juggi provided by the employer	7.2
Shelter home	17
Others	2.8

Lack of employment proof

Unfortunately, the ephemeral nature of their mode of employment does not allow a majority of the labour chowk workers to have any proof of employment. Of all the respondents, only 5.5% of them said that they have proof of employment.

Access to health and food

For health issues, most of the respondents said that they go to government hospitals to seek treatment. While 70.7% of the workers said that they go to government hospitals, 21.5% of the respondents said they go to private hospitals/clinics for treatment. Around 10% of them said that they just go to the drugstore to look for the right medicines. 1.2% of them said that they go to an NGO/Trust Hospital to seek treatment.

When asked about access to the Public Distribution System (PDS), 97% of them said that they do not have any access to the PDS. This lapse has led to normalized large-scale starvation in the labour chowks, with 46% of total respondents not being able to have three meals a day.

5

Placing Labour Chowk Workers in the Legal System

The narratives above highlight low wages, long working hours, and wage theft as the primary issues faced by a majority of workers. The Minimum Wages Act 1948, Payment of Wages Act 1936, the Equal Remuneration Act 1976, and the Payment of Bonus Act 1965 were the legal provisions available to address these issues to varying degrees earlier. The Code on Wages Act, 2019 consolidated the Minimum Wages Act 1948, Payment of Wages Act 1936, the Equal Remuneration Act 1976, and the Payment of Bonus Act 1965 into one code.

Unequal remuneration between men and women is the norm, where lower remuneration for women is justified by characterizing them as 'helpers'. While some directly-recruited migrant workers in organized construction sites can prove that they are employed by a particular builder, daily-wage workers from the labour chowk do not have such proof. A majority of them being either informal workers in organized workspaces or informal workers in unorganized workspaces adds to their exclusion from the legal structure.

This echoes the observations of Jan Breman (1999) that labour regulations—labour security, working hours, housing, safety at the workplace, etc.—were designed for the industrial working class in India. He also notes that the labour legislation was mainly designed to define the industrial procedures and to solve the disputes between employers and workers and to set up machinery charged with administration and registration, inspection, arbitration and adjudication, and other tasks exclusively concerned with labour and employment in the organized sector of the economy.

The design of rare progressive legislations such as the Building and Other Construction Workers (Regulation of Employment and Conditions of Service) Act, 1996 that considers the seasonality of employment is also incompatible with the lives of labour-chowk workers. Even though this law acknowledges the seasonality of the labour in the construction sector and allows any construction worker who has worked for 90 days in a year to be registered as a beneficiary under the state welfare boards, the beneficiaries also have to re-register themselves each year under the same state boards. The daily-wage workers who work seasonally in the construction sector are eligible to be beneficiaries under the act, but their migration patterns are so erratic that they do not work in the same state every year. They also lack the documents to prove that they have been working in the construction sector. Besides, the absence of trade unions working among the daily-wage migrant workers eliminates the option of being certified as a worker by the unions. The draft Code on Social Security (Central) Rules, 2020, (Chapter VII, 47) responding to the long-held demand for portability of social security, mention that when a building worker migrates from one state to another, he shall be entitled to get benefits from the board in whose jurisdiction he is currently working, and such board shall be responsible for providing such benefits to workers. However, this provision assumes that interstate migration is a linear process than circulation and undermines the essence of portability.

Further, the draft rules (Chapter VIII, 50 B) state that in order to be eligible for any benefit under any scheme(s) framed under the Code for any unorganized worker or any category or sub-category of an unorganized worker, the appropriate Government may notify specific condition(s) for eligibility, as deemed fit. For example, the BOCW boards in certain states do not accept self-declaration, despite the Act specifying that it is a valid proof of work. When each state government sets its own rules for eligibility, it creates confusion and leads to the rejection of eligible applicants. The rules also recommend the registration of workers under unorganized-sector workers social security boards through a web portal, which would lead to the exclusion of several migrant workers who do not even have access to mobile phones.

In addition to the violations of labour rights, the workers at the labour chowks are also excluded from the right to housing and subsequently from all the residential proof–based welfare provisions at the destination. A considerable number of workers who participated in the survey stay in night shelters. The night shelters in Delhi are established under the Delhi Urban Shelter Improvement Board Act (2010) aimed primarily at improving the living conditions in JJ clusters. The entry to the shelter homes is registered daily, depending on capacity. Each worker gets a mattress and a blanket. Some shelters also charge residents Rs. 10 per day. They are not given any designated place like a shelf to store their belongings while at the shelter. The families who migrate together prefer to live on the street as most of the shelters are sex-segregated. They also do not provide food or allow the residents to cook inside.

Even though the operational guidelines of scheme of shelters under the National Urban Livelihoods Mission (2013) direct the concerned authorities to map the sites where workers and urban poor are congregated, no such mapping has been undertaken yet. Ravi Srivastava (2020) has pointed out the exclusion of migrant workers also from subsidized public sector housing such as Pradhan Mantri Awas Yojana (PMAY), where beneficiaries are determined through BPL (Below Poverty Line) cards. Migrant workers often travel without documents because there is always a possibility of theft due to insecure housing. Hence, homeless migrants often do not have identity cards to prove their eligibility. Interstate migration, as in the case of Delhi labour chowks, also excludes the workers from availing state-specific schemes on housing. The same limitations apply to the provision of housing loans under the Building and Other Construction Workers (Regulation of Employment and Conditions of Service) Act, 1996.

It is often argued that the exclusion of workers from the legal structure is an implementation error. While acknowledging the power relations and bureaucratic incompetency, it is also important to recognize that the lived reality of a daily-wage migrant worker is often outside the imagination of the legal design intended to protect them. They are sidelined by a machinery that is mainly designed to redress the grievances of the formal-sector workers, and they are also kept out of the policies that are meant to ensure basic living conditions for the urban poor.

6

Spatial Inequalities

The lived realities of the workers, their narratives of harassment, theft, emotional traumas and the lack of secure space to sleep at night substantiate Breman's (1999) argument that informality extends beyond the economy to politics and governance. It is not only urban governance that excludes the migrants, but exclusion also manifests in the form of spatial inequality in cities. Spatial inequality broadly refers to the specific patterns that determine where diverse urban residents are able to live in a city-region and how it in turn determines the citizenship and belongingness in a city (Bhan and Jana, 2015).

Labour chowks located in the centre of the city, often physically proximate to bus stands, railway stations, or big construction projects represent these stark spatial inequalities neoliberal cities reproduce. Most of the workers at the Sarai Kale Khan labour chowk sleep on the concrete divider, whereas more permanent homeless populations use the footpath under the flyovers. This is a relatively secure space because it is roofed. Except for a narrow footpath to cross the roads, the rest of the spaces under flyovers are turned into beautiful gardens, fenced to prevent people from entering them. The workers are mobbed by the police into sleeping on the dividers. There are two large parks next to the labour chowks; however, the parks are guarded, and workers are not allowed to go inside. Map 1 shows that the shelters and the living spaces of workers get grievously low stakes in the city's public spaces. Even though there

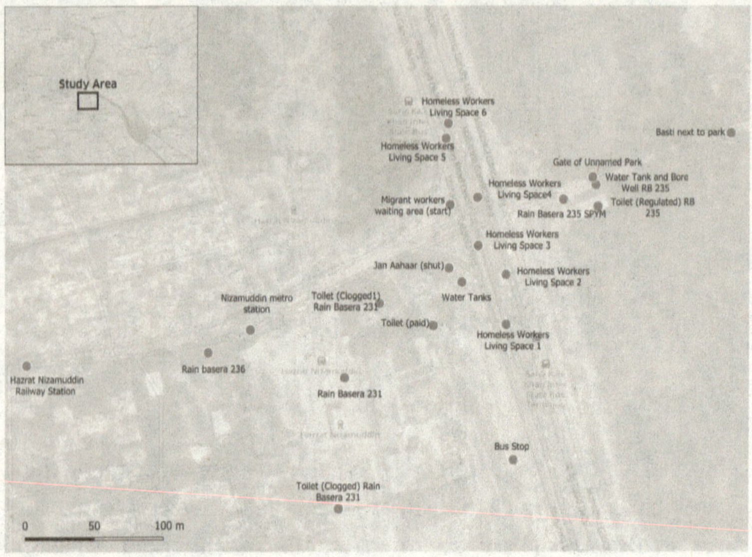

are toilets in the shelters, most of them are clogged and workers go to the open space next to the park to relieve themselves. The payment for using the paid toilet comes to Rs. 10–15 a day per person. One of the respondents said she prefers to buy biscuits or chips for her young children with that amount so that they stop crying for a few hours. The shelters do not have kitchens—one of the reasons why mothers prefer to live in the open, so that they can get a small gas cylinder and stove top to boil milk and water and cook for their children. The lack of safe shelter forces workers to leave their documents at home. Theft is rampant on the street, and the workers often lose their valuable documents. There were several workers we met at the Company Bagh labour chowk who lost the acknowledgement slip that is needed to collect the Aadhar card. Some of them were anxious to tell the officials that they had lost the slip. Homelessness and insecure housing subsequently exclude them from document-based welfare provisions. There are no primary health centres close to these spaces, even though the most vulnerable of the urban poor live in and around the labour chowks. There is no access to water; except for two shelter homes, none had a public tap. This spatial disproportionality in the geography of the city is lived through every day by the migrant workers. It is hence crucial to imagine services and welfare provisions of the urban poor spatially, inclusive of these informal and temporary spaces.

7

Discussions

The labour chowk is one of the few spaces in the city informally entitled to the circular migrant workers. It operates as a space in which one can find work and wait in till one does. Among the internal migrants in India, circular migrants are specifically vulnerable due to a number of reasons mentioned previously. The workers who come to the labour chowks do not have a permanent workplace, work schedule or a wage provider. The current study finds that most of the workers in Delhi are from other states. They are recruited for work in the neighbouring states of Delhi as well. This pattern of mobility excludes them from many of the state-specific schemes unlike other migrant workers.

The workers from the labour chowk are severely exploited at the workplace. There are multiple middlemen between the employers and the workers. Wage theft by these middlemen is rampant, and the bargaining power of workers in case of non-payment of wages or long working hours is low due to the lack of kin or family network at places so distant from home. Non-circular migrants, in spite of similar working conditions, may manage to build some local networks. Circular migrants move to a new place each time for short periods and are therefore unable to do so, making them specifically vulnerable to exploitation and wage theft. Finally, there is the threat of captivity and unbearable harassment at the workplace that each of these workers has faced at least once in their life.

The study also found that almost none of the workers we interacted with were part of trade unions. The organizations we interacted with that targeted migrant construction workers were able to enrol migrant workers living on rent and send children to school. However, a majority of the workers we met at the labour chowk do not have a permanent place to stay or any temporary proof of address. The model of membership-based unions is bound to fail in a situation where long term, consistent engagement is required from the workers. The trade unions are also stakeholders in elections and the migrant workers do not have voting rights in the destination states. This makes them an unwanted group with no stake in the political future of organizations.

The workers also lead a precarious work life in an unpredictable labour market. Work like the shaadi-party line is relatively better paid, but seasonal. Availability of work from labour chowks is also dependent on the demand for surplus labour.

The narratives of the workers tell us that the intersections of caste, gender, and ability, along with these vulnerabilities, give each of them a unique story of survival. The story of the inter-caste couple hiding from their partners and family tells us how the anonymity of the labour chowk gives them a place to hide in the crowd. At the same time, it also shows how toiling everyday becomes the only way to survive. Shivam's story tells us how unpredictable the life of a worker is. Despite being a hard worker and saving enough money, one accident was enough to push him to the streets. The failure of multiple institutions—a failed labour office that could not ensure minimum working hours, the failed banking system that could have kept his money safe, a failed health-care institution that could have ensured better medical care, and a failure of care-giving institutions that could ensure his recovery—reduced him to a beggar on street.

The story of Dhaniram and his family tells us how alarming the conditions in agrarian rural India are. The legal reforms to ease agriculture are undermined by the caste Hindus in political power. In this case, the family from an agrarian middle caste lost most of their land in the land consolidation process. The caste structure of their village is such that mere land ownership does not amount to an income from agriculture. The access to water bodies is controlled by the upper-caste people. Like Dhaniram, several other men from his village migrated to the labour chowk in Sarai Kale Khan.

Debt is another reason why people migrate. The conversations with Chunnilal's family demonstrate how traditional artisans are fraught with never-ending debt in rural India. The loss of livelihood due to larger changes in the political economy forces traditional artisans to take up low-skill construction work in the city.

Women are often the most marginalized. The labour chowks are predominantly occupied by men. Women who come to the labour chowk migrate with their families. The responsibilities of childcare, living in the street in harsh weather conditions, cooking and cleaning, along with working full time at the construction site, are burdens women exclusively bear. The lack of family shelter homes with a kitchen to cook food suitable for their children while they wait for work pushes them to live on the street instead. Once they get work, the responsibility of reproducing everyday life in difficult circumstances also falls on them. The absence of childcare institutions, along with the design of shelter homes targeting the single homeless population, fails to recognize the burdens of the female migrant population. Meena and Sheela's interview also talks about how various schemes for women and children imagine only stay-at-home mothers as their target. Pregnant women who are migrants do not have access to Anganwadis or creches.

Labour chowks located in the centre of the city, often physically proximate to bus stands, railway stations or big construction projects represent the stark spatial inequalities neoliberal cities reproduce. On the one hand, there are big buildings and big flyovers taking away more spaces while the workers have to confine to the dividers. There are also 'protected' arks and gardens around them, but all locked up and inaccessible. The labour camps are often located at the corners of the big societies being built, yet in the street the workers take turns for a safe sleep. This spatial disproportionality in the geography of the city is lived everyday by the migrant workers.

The field work for this report was carried out in late 2017, 2018, and early 2019, before the COVID-19 crisis struck. During this period, the labour laws in the country were going through a change, the four labour codes were under review; they were passed in 2020. The rules of the four labour codes are still undergoing changes at the time this report is being written. Several states issued ordinances during the first half of the lockdown, relaxing labour laws to encourage the ease of doing business (Sulfath and Sunilraj, 2021). Further, the economy was going through a period of increased unemployment prior to the lockdown. The impact of the pandemic on the informal workers, their wages, living conditions and working conditions is yet to be captured completely.

The crisis of the circular migrants was more visible in the first wave of the pandemic; thousands walked home and thousands who stayed back in cities had to stand in long queues to get a meal for themselves. The reality, however, was not far too different for the migrant workers prior to this crisis. The findings from the survey show that starvation was rampant among the workers prior to the lockdown, and they did not have access to primary health care, water, or sanitation facilities.

The discussions on migrant workers immediately after the lockdown have raised several questions about the country's economy and the ongoing agrarian crisis illustrating the root of the problem. This report put forward the following recommendations for areas that need immediate interventions in the destination states, the states that receive migrant workers.

Definitions and data

1. Rework the definitions of migration under the NSSO and census to accurately enumerate the scale of migration.
2. The Code on Occupational Safety, Health and Working Conditions (Chapter 1, section 2 (41)) specifies that the maximum

wages of the migrant worker should not exceed Rs. 18,000 per month in order to be considered a migrant worker. The wages are subsequently defined as constituting basic pay, retaining allowance and dearness allowance (Chapter 1 section 2 (88)). The code also lists out other related payments that should be excluded from the wage calculation. However, the draft rules of the Code on Social Security (2020) do not define how the monthly wage of a migrant worker is calculated. Much of the lower-income migrants are also short term–seasonal migrants who move for work on a seasonal basis (e.g., shaadi-party work) and live out of their savings for the rest of the year. They also do not strictly work for 8 hours a day; sometimes the working hours go up to 12–18 hours. The payments are higher in these cases, even though there is no consistency of employment throughout the year. It is implied that they do not have any proof of their wages, nor a breakdown of the wages as given in the code applicable in this case. It is important to have clear directives on how the wages are calculated and how it would be verified.

On labour rights and social security

3. The draft rules for the social security code (Chapter vii, 47) also mention that in cases where a building worker migrates from one state to another, he shall be entitled to get benefits from the board in whose jurisdiction he is currently working, and such board shall be responsible for providing such benefits to such workers. However, this is not the essence of portability. Specifically, in the case of migrant workers, each scheme should be portable both from the source state to the destination state and vice versa. Given the dropout rates of children of migrant workers, this has to be specified in the terms of the scheme on educational scholarship and other relevant schemes.

4. Subsequently, the draft rules (Chapter viii, 50 B) state that in order to be eligible for any benefit under any scheme(s)

framed under the Code for any unorganized worker or any category or sub-category of an unorganized worker, the appropriate Government may notify specific condition(s) for eligibility, as deemed fit. This goes against the essence of portability and is likely to result in the constitution of different rules in each state for registration. Further, many states currently do not accept self-declaration as a legitimate document to register oneself as a beneficiary of the BOCW Act. There should be a standardized format for eligibility across states as state governments can use the vagueness of the code and rules to continue demanding proof of work for registration.

5. Even though the draft rules of the Code on Social Security (2020) recommend the institutionalization of labour helplines for the unorganized-sector workers, it does not mandate a separate helpline for the interstate migrant workers. The labour helplines should be designed in an accessible way and have multi-lingual operators to help the migrant workers.

6. Presently, there are no legal consequences for the contractor/employer not registering the workers under welfare boards. It should be mandatory for each worksite employing workers beyond a specified limit to have a definite number of compulsory registration drives with the welfare board each year. The participation of workers, however, should be voluntary.

7. Migrant-worker facilitation centres should be opened near railway stations and bus stations at major destination states. A system where workers can report and document details of their work (where they are taken, what is the name of the employer, what are the wage and working hours agreed between them) at the facilitation centres should be instituted. This can serve as a reference for any possible disputes and a general mechanism to ensure the accountability of the employers.

8. For general registration drives, the labour departments should be directed to collaborate with civil society organizations (CSOs), trade unions, or any other relevant body, to ensure

that arbitrary certification of work is not demanded from the workers to be registered as a beneficiary under different schemes.

9. The draft rules for the Code on Social Security, 2020 (Chapter viii, 50 2B) state that 'For availing any benefit under any of the social security schemes, an unorganized worker or a gig worker or platform worker shall be required to be registered on the portal'. Evidence suggests that the migrant workers are often not covered in these kinds of registration until and unless a registration drive is undertaken. Civil society organizations and trade unions should have the authorization to register workers with different boards.

10. Non-payment of wages is currently a civil liability and not criminal liability under the wage code. It is punishable with a fine up to Rs. 50,000. The penalty of imprisonment as per the previous version of the Act should be restored.

On the rights of women and children

11. All the drafts of labour codes and their rules should avoid using male pronouns for workers.

12. Childcare should be provisioned for all the hours that the parents work at organized workspaces such as construction sites.

13. There should be strong regulations to prevent employers from refusing to hire workers with children, and creche facilities should be sufficient to cover all children of eligible age.

14. While the draft rules of the Code on Social Security (2020) specify the duration of the break that can be taken by nursing mothers, it does not specify the distance of the creche from the workplace. Rule no. 38 states: 'An extra sufficient period, depending upon the distance to be covered, shall be allowed for the purpose of journey to and from the creche or the place where the children are left by women while on duty, provided that such extra period shall not be of less than 5 minutes and more than 15 minutes duration'. However, rule no. 39 only

states that the crèche facility shall be located within the establishment or at an appropriate distance from the establishment such that it is easily accessible to the women employees including a woman employee working from home. It does not specify the distance of the creches from workplaces. Nursing breaks should be exclusive of the commute time, provided creches can be physically located far from the worksite or rule no. 39 should specify the limit of the distance between the creche and the workspace.

15. Creche facilities in smaller worksites are not covered under the mandates of the law. Workers have an informal system of childcare where they babysit rotationally. The law must explore this option and institutionalize this arrangement for smaller informal worksites. The employer should be made liable for paying the wages of the worker who is taking the responsibility of childcare each day.

16. Rajiv Gandhi National Creche Scheme for working mothers must be extended to worksites and labour chowks. Mobile creches must be included in the scheme. The information on the exact locations of these creches must be provided at the proposed facilitation centres.

17. Admission in the middle of the school year must be permitted.

18. Jan Ahar centres must be opened to provide cheap and nutritious food for the workers. Milk and baby food must be made available at the Jan Ahar centres.

Housing rights

19. Initiate the mapping exercises necessary for building new shelters as prescribed under the schemes of NULM.

20. Amend the Delhi Urban Improvement Board Act, 2010 to include interstate migrant workers. Build more shelter homes around the labour chowk. The shelter homes should be designed to accommodate migrating families and equipped with childcare facilities and a community kitchen.

21. Implement the draft National Urban Rental Housing Policy, 2015. Build separate living spaces for migrant labourers under 'need-based rental housing' and other provisions.

Bibliography

Bhan, Gautam. *In the Public's Interest: Evictions, Citizenship and Inequality in Contemporary Delhi.* Athens, GA: University of Georgia Press, 2016.

Breman, Jan. *On Pauperism in Present and Past.* New Delhi: Oxford University Press, 2016.

Breman, Jan. *Outcast Labour in Asia: Circulation and Informalization of the Workforce at the Bottom of the Economy.* Oxford: Oxford University Press, 2010.

Breman, Jan. "The Study of Industrial Labour in Post-Colonial India—the Informal Sector: A Concluding Review." *Contributions to Indian Sociology* 33, no. 1-2 (1999): 407–31. https://doi.org/10.1177/006996679903300117.

Delhi School of Social Work. Rep. *Mapping of Construction Workers in National Capital Territory of Delhi,* 2009.

Deshingkar, P. & Akter, S. 2009. "Migration and Human Development in India," *Human Development Research Papers (2009 to present) HDRP-2009-13,* Human Development Report Office (HDRO), United Nations Development Programme (UNDP), revised Apr 2009.

"Draft of the Code on Social Security (Central) Rules, 2020." Ministry of Law and Justice, November 13, 2020. https://labour.gov.in/sites/default/files/DRAFTCOSSRULES2020NOV.pdf

Jayaram, Nivedita. "Protection of Workers' Wages in India: An Analysis of the Labour Code on Wages, 2019." *Economic and Political Weekly* 54, no. 49 (December 2019).

Korra, Vijay. "Short-Duration Migration in India." Essay. In *India Migration Report 2011: Migration, Identity and Conflict*, edited by S. I. Rajan. Routledge, 2011.

National Commission for Enterprises in the Unorganized Sector, (NCEUS). Rep. *Report on Conditions of Work and Promotion of Livelihoods in the Unorganized Sector*

"Operational Guidelines for Scheme of Shelter for Urban Homeless, NULM." Ministry of Housing and Urban Affairs. August, 2013.   http://mohua.gov.in/upload/uploadfiles/files/7NULM-SUH-Guidelines.pdf

People's Union of Democratic Rights. "Code on Wage Bill 2017-A Proposed Legislation Violating the Rights of the Workers." Countercurrents, November 8, 2017. https://countercurrents.org/2017/11/code-on-wage-bill-2017-a-proposed-legislation-violating-the-rights-of-workers/.

Singh, C. S. K. "Daily Labour Market in Delhi: Structure and Behaviour." *Economic and Political Weekly* 37, no. 9 (2002): 884–89. http://www.jstor.org/stable/4411815.

Srivastava, Ravi. Publication. *Internal Migration in India: An Overview of Its Features, Trends and Policy Challenges*.

Srivastava, Ravi. Rep. *Vulnerable Internal Migrants in India and Portability of Social Security and Entitlements*. New Delhi: Institute for Human Development, 2020.

Sulfath, Jenny, and Balu Sunilraj. "Covid-19 Crisis Exposes India's Neglect of Informal Workers." NewsClick, May 12, 2020. https://www.newsclick.in/Covid-19-Crisis-Exposes-India-Neglect-Informal-Workers.

"The Building and Other Construction Workers (Regulation of Employment and Conditions of Service) Act, 1996 (No. 27 of 1996)". Ministry of Labour & Employment. August 19, 1996. https://www.indiacode.nic.in/bitstream/123456789/1989/1/A1996__27.pdf

"The Code on Wages, 2019 (No.29 of 2019)." eGazzette. Ministry of Law and Justice, August 8, 2019. https://egazette.nic.in/WriteReadData/2019/210356.pdf

"The Delhi Urban Shelter Improvement Board Act, 2010." Department of Urban Development, Government of National Capital Territory of Delhi; April 01, 2010. https://delhishelterboard.in/main/wp-content/uploads/2012/02/DUSIB-ACT-2010.pdf

Thorat, Y.S.P, and H. Jones. *Remittance Needs and Opportunities in India.* New Delhi, India: NABARD Rural Finances Institutions Programme (RFIP), German Development Cooperation (GIZ), 2011.

Vigyan Foundation. Rep. *Labour Posts in Allahabad: An Insight into the Working Conditions of the Migrant Workers in Allahabad.* Action Aid India, 2010.

Vigyan Foundation. Rep. *Labour Posts in Lucknow: An Insight into the Working Conditions of the Migrant Workers in Lucknow.* Action Aid India, 2010.

Vigyan Foundation. Rep. *Labour Posts in Agra: An Insight into the Working Conditions of the Migrant Workers in Agra.* Action Aid India, 2010.

Working People's Charter. "Craftily Written Labour Codes Exclude Millions, Pay Little Heed to Equality." The Wire, July 2019. https://thewire.in/labour/cabinet-passes-labour-codes-wages-occupational-safety.

About the Authors

Jenny Sulfath is an Assistant Manager (Communications) at Digital Empowerment Foundation and was a Senior Researcher at Centre for Equity Studies, New Delhi from June 2017 till November 2020. She has an MA and MPhil in Women's Studies from TISS, Mumbai.

Shirin Choudhary is an International Climate Protection Fellow at Alexander von Humboldt-Stiftung, Berlin Germany and was a Researcher at Centre for Equity Studies, New Delhi from July 2019 till November 2020. They hold a master's degree in Human Rights and Humanitarian Action from Sciences Po, Paris.

The authors share an interest in poetry, cats and reading fiction. Shirin likes to play video games. Jenny enjoys watching movies.

Follow them on Instagram at @jennysulfath and @lonefoxdancing.

www.ingramcontent.com/pod-product-compliance
Lightning Source LLC
LaVergne TN
LVHW031326190726
843493LV00013B/3049